Edexcel GCSE (9–1) Spanish
Grammar & Translation Workbook

John Halksworth, Ian Kendrick, Ben Konopinski and Tracy Traynor

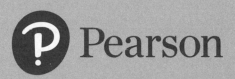

How to use your Grammar and Translation Workbook

This workbook is divided into three sections:

1. Grammar and translation

This section provides lots of useful practice and support as you work through ¡Viva! Edexcel GCSE Spanish. Master key grammar points with the help of clear explanations and examples followed by focussed grammar and translation exercises.

Look out for links to pages in your ¡Viva! Edexcel GCSE Spanish Higher or Foundation Student Book, for more on a particular grammar point:

» Foundation pp. 10–11
» Higher pp. 8–9

(Note: the grammar points in this workbook aren't just linked to the topics where you first encounter them in the Student Book, though – they cover a wider range of vocabulary to give you the confidence to be able to understand and use grammar in lots of different contexts.)

Exercises and explanations marked with the symbol 🄷 are aimed at users of the Higher Student Book. Why not give them a try?

2. Translation in practice

Brush up on useful strategies to help you tackle translations before putting into practice all of the grammar, vocabulary and translation skills you have learned, with this bank of translation activities covering all of the different topics you will need to know for your exams. This is a great way to revise grammar and vocabulary at the end of your course (and you'll need to tackle translation questions in your Edexcel GCSE Reading and Writing exams, so this is great practice!)

3. Verb tables

A handy list of regular and irregular verbs in the key tenses you'll need to know, to refer to whenever you need!

Tips

Look out for the following tips to help you as you work through the book:

 Handy hints to help you with grammar.

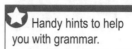 Clues to help you translate a specific word or phrase.

💡 Useful strategies to remember for your translations.

Answers

Answers to all of the exercises and model translations for every translation task are available on our online *ActiveLearn Digital Service* – just ask your teacher who will be able to access these. Teachers, you'll need to visit www.pearsonschools.co.uk to order these (at no cost).

Published by Pearson Education Limited, 80 Strand, London, WC2R 0RL

www.pearsonschoolsandfecolleges.co.uk

Copies of official specifications for all Edexcel qualifications may be found on the website: www.edexcel.com

Text © Pearson Education Limited 2017
Edited by Charonne Prosser and Linda Byrne
Designed by Tek-Art, East Grinstead, West Sussex
Typeset by Tek-Art, East Grinstead, West Sussex
Original illustrations © Pearson Education Limited 2017
Illustrated by Tek-Art, Beehive Illustration, KJA Artists and John Hallett
Cover photo © Alamy/Kevin George

First published 2017

20 19 18 17
10 9 8 7 6 5 4 3 2

British Library Cataloguing in Publication Data
A catalogue record for this book is available from the British Library

ISBN 978 1 292 13330 0

Printed in Slovakia by Neografia

Acknowledgements
We would like to thank Teresa Álvarez, Sarah Brierley, Clare Dobson, Penny Fisher, James Hodgson, Nicola Lester, Daniela Vega López, Abigail Watson and Melissa Wilson for their invaluable help in the development of this book.

A note from the publisher
In order to ensure that this resource offers high-quality support for the associated Pearson qualification, it has been through a review process by the awarding body. This process confirms that this resource fully covers the teaching and learning content of the specification or part of a specification at which it is aimed. It also confirms that it demonstrates an appropriate balance between the development of subject skills, knowledge and understanding, in addition to preparation for assessment.

Endorsement does not cover any guidance on assessment activities or processes (e.g. practice questions or advice on how to answer assessment questions) included in the resource nor does it prescribe any particular approach to the teaching or delivery of a related course.

While the publishers have made every attempt to ensure that advice on the qualification and its assessment is accurate, the official specification and associated assessment guidance materials are the only authoritative source of information and should always be referred to for definitive guidance.

Pearson examiners have not contributed to any sections in this resource relevant to examination papers for which they have responsibility.

Examiners will not use endorsed resources as a source of material for any assessment set by Pearson.

Endorsement of a resource does not mean that the resource is required to achieve this Pearson qualification, nor does it mean that it is the only suitable material available to support the qualification, and any resource lists produced by the awarding body shall include this and other appropriate resources.

This work is produced by Pearson Education and is not endorsed by any trademark owner referenced in the publication.

Contents

Nouns Gender and number

» *Foundation pp. 132–133*
» *Higher pp. 138–139*

 Nouns are naming words: they give names to people, things and abstract concepts like ideas or feelings, e.g. 'Karen', 'pen', 'happiness'.

Gender

In Spanish, all nouns have a gender: they are all masculine or feminine. (This includes things as well as people.) It is important to know a noun's gender because this tells you:

- which form of the **article** to use with it (*un* or *una, el* or *la, los* or *las*)
- the endings for **adjectives** that go with the noun.

> ⭐ For more on articles and adjectives, see pp. 6–7 and 8–17.

The gender of many nouns is obvious from the ending: **–o** nouns are usually <u>masculine</u> and **–a** nouns are usually <u>feminine</u>.

	singular	plural
masculine	el chic**o** el libr**o**	los chic**os** los libr**os**
feminine	la chic**a** la regl**a**	las chic**as** las regl**as**

There are, however, some exceptions:

- common masculine words ending in **–a**: *el mapa, el día* and lots of words ending in **–ma**, e.g. *el problema, el sistema, el clima, el programa*
- common feminine words ending in **–o**: *la mano, la radio, la foto, la moto* (note, too, **el** *agua* and **el** *área*: *agua* and *área* are feminine, but *el* is used instead of *la* because *la agua* and *la área* are too hard to say).

For nouns ending in other letters, there are some patterns to help you.

- Nouns with the following endings are usually masculine:

  –ma (*el idioma*)   **–or** (*el color*)

  The days of the week are also all masculine.

- Nouns with the following endings are usually feminine:

  –ción (*la natación*)   **–iz** (*la nariz*)   **–ie** (*la serie*)
  –dad (*la felicidad*)   **–sis** (*la crisis*)   **–umbre** (*la costumbre*)

For other words, you have to learn the gender when you learn the noun. A good way to do this is to learn each new noun with its definite article, e.g. **el** *salón*, **la** *catedral*.

Plural nouns

You form the plural of nouns ending in a vowel by adding **–s**: *los chicos*. For nouns ending in a consonant you add **–es**: *las catedrales*. (An exception to this is days of the week ending in **–s**: *el lunes/los lunes*.) Note that if the noun has an accent on the last syllable in the singular, this does not carry through to the plural: *el salón/los salones*.

Nouns referring to people

- Most nouns referring to men are masculine (e.g. *el hombre*) and most nouns referring to women are feminine (e.g. *la mujer*).
- When talking about a group that includes a mixture of men and women, you use masculine forms.
- When talking about jobs or other ways of describing people, you often need different forms of the noun for boys/men and girls/women, e.g. **el** *camarero* and **la** *camarera*.
- Sometimes the noun doesn't change – only the article does. This happens with nouns of professions ending in **–ante** and **–ista**: *el/la estudiante, el/la recepcionista*.
- If the masculine noun ends in a consonant, you generally add **–a** to the end to make it feminine: *el diseñador/la diseñadora, el inglés/la inglesa*.

1 Write the correct form of the article.

1	_____ jardines	5	_____ estudiante	9	_____ tienda
2	_____ universidad	6	_____ mapa	10	_____ profesor
3	_____ foto	7	_____ combinación	11	_____ camarero
4	_____ flores	8	_____ programas	12	_____ coches

> Remember – what gender are most nouns ending in **–a**?

2 Circle the noun in each sentence. Identify whether it is masculine (m) or feminine (f) and singular (s) or plural (pl).

1 El hombre es guapo. _____

2 Vio a los alumnos. _____

3 Me interesan las matemáticas. _____

4 Tocamos la guitarra pero no me gusta. _____

H 3 Complete these sentences with appropriate nouns from the box.

opción	deporte	aplicación	semana	periódicos
autobús	novelas	niños	consumo	fanática

⭐ You won't need to use all the words.

1 Reducir el _____ eléctrico es la única _____ .

2 Me gusta leer las _____ pero no me interesan los _____ .

3 Leo las noticias a través de una _____ en mi móvil cuando estoy esperando el _____ .

4 El treinta por ciento de los _____ gasta más de veinte euros a la _____ .

4 Rewrite these sentences making the nouns plural. Then translate your sentences into English.

⭐ Make sure your translation sounds natural in English.

1 Me dio un caramelo y una naranja. _____

2 Conocí a un hombre y a una mujer. _____

3 Compraron el mapa y la radio. _____

5 Translate these sentences into Spanish.

Remember that you need the definite article when you are talking about things you like/dislike.

1 I like films but I'm not interested in cartoons. _____

2 I buy vegetables and a cake at the market. _____

This also needs the definite article.

3 Last winter I went to the mountains. _____

6 Translate this passage into Spanish.

Use No debo.

My friends and I are going to spend a few days in Mexico. The weather is very sunny there. I'm going to meet them at the railway station tomorrow at 10. Ana is bringing a map. I mustn't forget my phone because I want to listen to some songs on the train.

_____

Articles are used with nouns. In Spanish, the words for 'the' (the definite article) and 'a' (an) and 'some' (the indefinite article) change according to the gender and number of the noun they are with.

Definite articles

	singular	plural
masculine	**el** chic**o** (the boy)	**los** chic**os** (the boys)
feminine	**la** chic**a** (the girl)	**las** chic**as** (the girls)

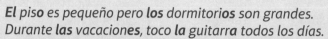

*El piso es pequeño pero **los** dormitorios son grandes.*   **The** house is small but **the** bedrooms are big.
*Durante **las** vacaciones, toco **la** guitarra todos los días.*   During **the** holidays, I play **the** guitar every day.

You use the definite article in Spanish in the same way as you do in English, with the following exceptions. Here *el/la/los/las* is used where you wouldn't use 'the' in English:

• opinions:	*Me chiflan **las** telenovelas.*	I love soap operas.
• parts of the body:	*Tiene **el** pelo castaño.*	She/he has brown hair.
• days of the week:	***el** lunes*	on Monday
• times:	*Son **las** dos.*	It's two o'clock.
• abstract nouns:	***la** paz*	peace
• languages:	***el** francés*	French
• school subjects:	***las** matemáticas*	Maths

Lo

Spanish also has a neuter form of 'the' – *lo* – which you use to describe 'the ... thing / part'. *Lo* is used with an adjective (not a noun) and the adjective form doesn't change.

The following expressions with *lo* + adjective are particularly useful:

*¡**Lo bueno** es que todos mis amigos están aquí!*	The **good thing** is that all my friends are here!
***Lo malo** es que voy a llegar tarde.*	The **bad thing** is that I am going to arrive late.
***Lo mejor** fue cuando vi el partido de fútbol.*	The **best part** was when I saw the football match.
***Lo peor** fue el tiempo.*	The **worst thing** was the weather.

Indefinite articles

	singular	plural
masculine	**un** chic**o** (a boy)	**unos** chic**os** (some boys)
feminine	**una** chic**a** (the girl)	**unas** chic**as** (some girls)

*Compré **una** falda roja y **unas** botas negras.*   I bought **a** red skirt and **some** black boots.
*Tiene **un** perro y **unos** peces.*   He has **a** dog and **some** fish.

You use the indefinite article in Spanish in the same way as in English, with one exception. When talking about jobs, *un/una* is not used where you would use 'a/an' in English:

Es policía.   He's a police officer.

When a group has at least one male member, you use the <u>masculine plural</u> form of the article and noun. So *los/unos profesores* could refer to a group of male teachers, or to a group of male <u>and</u> female teachers.

1 Put these words under the correct article heading.

hermana	series policíacas	ojos	serpientes
laboratorios	telediario	playa	programa de deportes

⭐ Many nouns ending in *–ma* are masculine.

el	la	los	las

2 Circle the nouns which **don't** go with the article each time.

1 **un**   zoo   partido de fútbol   niña   comedias   recepcionista   gato

2 **una**   bocadillos   mañana   actriz   cocina   cara   libro

3 **unos**   clientes   zapatos   documentales   vídeos   barrio   amigas

4 **unas**   verduras   churros   telenovelas   tiendas   restaurante   camisas

> ⭐ Look at the section on nouns on p. 4 to work out whether nouns are masculine or feminine to decide which article you need. Look up the word in a dictionary if you aren't sure.

3 Choose the correct form to complete each sentence.

1 Me gusta *la / el / las* chaqueta a rayas.

2 Llevó *unas / unos / los* medias azul oscuro.

3 ¿Cómo es *un / unas / una* buen amigo?

4 A Javier le gusta leer *el / las / una* revistas.

5 Fui a *uno / los / el* laboratorios.

6 En mi insti hay *un / una / unas* aulas.

7 Mi madre tiene *un / el / lo* pelo rubio.

8 *El / La / Lo* bueno es que hace sol.

4 Read each sentence. Are there any articles missing? Add in the correct article where necessary, then translate these sentences into English.

1 Me gustan documentales. ....

....

2 Compré botas moradas. ....

....

3 Mi madre es diseñadora. ....

....

H 4 Malo es que me duele cabeza. ....

....

> ⭐ Remember: sometimes you need an article in Spanish when you wouldn't use one in English, and vice versa.

5 Translate these sentences into Spanish.

1 I have a sister and a brother.

....

2 I like ice cream and I love pop music.

....

3 On Saturday I bought some jeans and some boots.

....

> Remember that you include the definite article when giving your opinon about things.

H **6** Translate this passage into Spanish.

> [Use *Hace* ...]

I really like spending the summer holidays in Spain, but I don't like hotels. I prefer to rent an apartment or a country house. A year ago, I visited Sitges with a friend. On Saturday, we went to the beach. I swam in the sea, then at two o'clock we went to a café. The best thing was the churros. They were fantastic!

> [Use *Lo* ...]   [masculine or feminine?]

....

....

....

....

G Adjectives are describing words. You use them to describe a noun, a person or a thing.

Agreement

Adjectives <u>agree</u> with the noun they describe. This means that the ending depends on whether the noun is masculine or feminine, singular or plural. Learn the different patterns here:

adjective ends in	masculine singular	feminine singular	masculine plural	feminine plural
-o/a	pequeñ**o**	pequeñ**a**	pequeñ**os**	pequeñ**as**
-e	grand**e**	grand**e**	grand**es**	grand**es**
-consonant	azul	azul	azul**es**	azul**es**
-or/ora	hablad**or**	hablad**ora**	hablad**ores**	hablad**oras**
-ista	optim**ista**	optim**ista**	optim**istas**	optim**istas**

*mi dormitori**o** es **pequeño***   my bedroom is **small**

Colour adjectives generally follow these rules of agreement, but there are some exceptions.

- *Naranja*, *rosa* and *violeta* often do not change, but some speakers add an –s with plural nouns.
- When *claro* (light) and *oscuro* (dark) follow a colour, they always take the masculine form:
  *un**os** calcetines azul **claro**, unas medias azul **oscuro***

Adjectives of nationality agree with the noun. Those ending in a vowel usually follow the regular pattern, but they follow different patterns if they end in a consonant. They do not start with a capital letter in Spanish.

adjective ends in	masculine singular	feminine singular	masculine plural	feminine plural
-o	italian**o**	italian**a**	italian**os**	italian**as**
-l	español	español**a**	español**es**	español**as**
-n	alemán	aleman**a**	aleman**es**	aleman**as**
-s	inglés	ingles**a**	ingles**es**	ingles**as**
-í or -ú	marroquí	marroquí	marroqu**íes**	marroqu**íes**

*los chic**os** argentin**os***   the Argentinian boys

Position

Unlike English, adjectives in Spanish usually come <u>after</u> the noun: *una persona **habladora***   a talkative person

Some adjectives, however, come <u>before</u> the noun, for example:

- *mucho, poco*
- *primero, segundo, próximo, último*

Some adjectives can be used before the noun, but have a short form when they are used before masculine singular nouns:

primero > primer	bueno > buen	alguno > algún	grande > gran*
tercero > tercer	malo > mal	ninguno > ningún	*before all singular nouns

1 Choose the correct form of the adjective.

1 Belén tiene el pelo *largo / larga*.
2 La sopa está *rico / rica*.
3 Mis padres son muy *inteligente / inteligentes*.
4 Tengo los ojos *marrón / marrones*.
5 Mis amigas son *español / españolas*.
6 Anna es muy *trabajadora / trabajador*.

2 Underline the adjective in each sentence. Is it in the correct position? If not, where should it go? Write the sentence out correctly.

1 Javier tiene los grises ojos. _____
2 El chico delgado es mi hermano. _____
3 En mi ciudad hay unos caros restaurantes. _____
4 Hay unos simpáticos chicos en mi clase. _____
5 Viven en una casa muy grande con su familia. _____
6 Los ambiciosos chicos son muy trabajadores. _____

3 Complete this table with the correct form of the adjective and the meaning.

singular		plural		English meaning
masculine	feminine	masculine	feminine	
pesimista				pessimistic
trabajador			trabajadoras	
	fiel			loyal
			gordas	fat
importante		importantes		
francés			francesas	

4 Write the correct form of the adjective in brackets.

1 Los chicos son muy _____ (*guapo*).

2 Mi insti es _____ (*antiguo*).

3 Me gustan las matemáticas pero no son _____ (*fácil*).

4 Los programas de deportes son _____ (*entretenido*).

5 El dibujo es bastante _____ (*interesante*).

6 La profesora es _____ (*irlandés*).

7 Victor es un _____ (*bueno*) amigo.

8 Fue un _____ (*grande*) día.

Think about whether you need an accent or not when you make the adjective agree with the noun.

5 Complete each sentence with the correct form of the noun and adjective given in brackets, in the correct position.

1 Son _____ (*delicious biscuits*).

2 Tengo _____ (*a black cat*).

3 Son _____ (*optimistic boys*).

4 Escribí a mi _____ (*English aunt*).

Think about the adjective endings. Masculine or feminine? Singular or plural?

6 Translate these sentences into Spanish.

1 José is shy and Ana is silly. _____

2 My uncles are Spanish. _____

3 She has long hair and blue eyes. _____

H 7 Translate this passage into Spanish.

Which word for 'short' do you need here?

Mr Gómez is very tall and quite fat. He has black hair and brown eyes. He's Mexican. His daughter Gabriela is short. She has long brown hair and green eyes. She's shy but kind. They live in a comfortable house with a big garden.

Which word for 'brown' do you need here?

_____

_____

_____

_____

Adjectives Possessive adjectives

» Foundation p. 46
» Higher p. 50

(G) In Spanish, possessive adjectives (the words for 'my', 'your', 'his', etc.) <u>agree</u> with the nouns they describe. This means that a different form may be used depending on whether the noun is masculine or feminine and singular or plural.

singular noun		plural noun		English meaning
masculine	feminine	masculine	feminine	
mi		mi**s**		my
tu		tu**s**		your (singular)
su		su**s**		his/her/its/ your (polite singular)
nuestr**o**	nuestr**a**	nuestr**os**	nuestr**as**	our
vuestr**o**	vuestr**a**	vuestr**os**	vuestr**as**	your (plural)
su		su**s**		their/ your (polite plural)

*Canto karaoke con **mis** amigos.*
__Su__ pasión es el tenis.

I sing karaoke with **my** friends.
His passion is tennis.

1 **Complete each set with the correct possessive adjectives.**

1 **mi** abuelo, _____ abuela, _____ abuelos, mis abuelas

2 **tu** hermano, _____ hermana, tus hermanos, _____ hermanas

3 **su** móvil, _____ cámara, _____ fotos, _____ aplicaciones

4 **nuestro** perro, nuestros conejos, _____ cobaya, _____ tortugas

5 **vuestros** caramelos, _____ pizza, _____ bocadillo, _____ naranjas

6 **sus** bicicletas, _____ coche, _____ trenes, _____ avión

2 **Choose the correct possessive adjective to complete each sentence.**

1 Me gusta chatear con *mis / su* amigos.

2 Alba y *su / sus* hermano me mandan mensajes.

3 Mi hermano y yo salimos los viernes con *mis / nuestras* primas.

4 Me gustan *tu / tus* pantalones.

5 Javier organiza *su / sus* cosas.

6 ¿Queréis compartir *vuestras / vuestro* vídeo favorito?

⭐ Remember: the possessive adjective agrees with the noun it describes (in gender and number), <u>not</u> with the subject.

3 Mateo is introducing himself and his family. Complete the sentences with the correct possessive adjectives.

Soy Mateo. **1** _____ deporte favorito es la escalada. Todo esto es **2** _____ equipo de escalada y estas son **3** _____ botas.

Mira mi hermano, Julián. **4** _____ pasión es la tecnología. Esos son **5** _____ videojuegos y ese es **6** _____ móvil. ¿Quieres ver **7** _____ fotos? ¡Tiene muchas!

¡Foto divertida! Mi padrastro y yo estamos en la playa. Mira **8** _____ barco y **9** _____ camisetas. ¡Qué guay!

4 Complete each sentence with the most logical possessive adjective. Then translate the sentences into English.

1 Mateo va a un instituto mixto con _____ hermana.

2 Estudiamos química con _____ amigos.

3 Trabajo con _____ equipo.

4 ¿Te gusta _____ insti?

5 Translate these sentences into Spanish.

1 Our dad is very strict.

2 Where are your brothers, Ben?

3 I go out with my friends.

Think about who's speaking and what possessive adjective you need. Then think about the noun: is it masculine or feminine? Is it singular or plural?

Remember this verb is irregular in the 'I' form of the present tense. Use the verb tables on pp. 124–128 if you need to check.

6 Translate this passage into Spanish.

My passion is taking photos. Look at some photos of my family. My parents are on the beach with my brothers. And this is my sister. She lives in London with her husband and their daughters. Their house is awesome! What about you? What are your favourite activities?

Which adjective could you use here?

Adjectives Demonstrative adjectives

>> Foundation p. 96
>> Higher p. 102

(G) Demonstrative adjectives are used to indicate a particular thing: 'this …', 'that …', 'that … over there'. In English, you use 'this' / 'these' and 'that' / 'those' to distinguish between things that are near you (here) and away from you (there). Spanish has three categories:

- near you (here)
- away from you or near the person you are talking to (there)
- further away (over there).

These words go <u>before</u> the noun and agree with the noun in gender and number.

singular		plural		English meaning
masculine	feminine	masculine	feminine	
este cuadro	esta revista	estos cuadros	estas revistas	this … / these …
ese cuadro	esa revista	esos cuadros	esas revistas	that … / those …
aquel cuadro	aquella revista	aquellos cuadros	aquellas revistas	that … / those … over there

*Prefiero **ese** coche pero **aquel** coche es más barato.*   I prefer **that** car but **that** car **over there** is cheaper.

Demonstrative adjectives can also be used to talk about time, to distinguish between events in the present and those in the recent or distant past.

***Ese** año fuimos de vacaciones a Mallorca, pero **este** año vamos a ir a Francia.*
That year we went on holiday to Mallorca, but **this** year we are going to go to France.

1 Write the correct form of the appropriate demonstrative adjective.

1 this/these: _____ amigas / _____ globos / _____ ordenador / _____ regla

2 that/those over there: _____ perro / _____ mochilas / _____ pizza / _____ coches

3 that/those: _____ queso / _____ caramelos / _____ cosas / _____ corbata

2 Translate these sentences into Spanish.

> Remember – you only need one word for 'that … over there'.

1 I don't want that skirt – I want that skirt over there.

_____

2 These books are blue and those are green.

_____

3 That dog over there is bigger than these dogs.

_____

> ★ Think carefully about agreement.

(H) 3 Translate this passage into Spanish.

I want some tomatoes – those tomatoes over there, please. And these oranges and those bananas. Last week I bought that bread over there. It was delicious! I'm going to take it and this cheese and that bottle of wine, too.

> Ser or estar?

> You'll need an object pronoun here

_____

_____

_____

_____

Adjectives Indefinite adjectives

» *Foundation p. 76*
» *Higher p. 83*

G You use **indefinite adjectives** to talk about people or things in a general way, without being specific: 'some', 'each', 'all'. In Spanish these words agree with the noun they accompany in gender (feminine/masculine) and number (singular/plural), taking the endings **–o**, **–a**, **–os**, **–as**.
Useful adjectives include:

cierto	certain	*mismo*	same	*otro*	other, another
demasiado	too much, too many	*mucho*	a lot of	*todo*	all, every

An exception is *cada* ('each', 'every'), which doesn't change.
Algún is slightly irregular in the masculine singular: *algún* (m), *alguna* (f).
Indefinite adjectives come <u>before</u> the noun they describe.

*Vamos al cine el **mismo** día.*   We're going to the cinema on the **same** day.
*¿Tiene **otros** pasteles?*   Do you have **other** cakes?

1 Write the gender (m) or (f) of these indefinite adjectives and whether each is singular (s) or plural (pl).

mismas ....   cada ....   otra ....   todas ....

muchos ....   algún ....   cierto ....   demasiada ....

2 Complete these sentences.

1 .... (*Certain*) películas son buenas pero .... (*others*) son aburridas.

2 Me interesan .... (*all*) los deportes.

3 Hay .... (*a lot of*) gente en el supermercado.

4 .... (*Some*) día va a viajar a los Estados Unidos.

5 ¿Puede darme .... (*some other*) manzanas?

> You need the definite article after the word for 'all' in Spanish.

> You don't need a separate word for 'some' here – it is implied in the word for 'other' in Spanish.

3 Translate these sentences into Spanish.

1 There are too many boys in the team.

....

2 We like the same TV programmes.

....

3 They go to the park every day.

....

> ⭐ Remember that indefinite adjectives come <u>before</u> the noun they describe.

> Masculine or feminine?

> You can say this in two ways. Remember, one of them must be followed by the definite article.

H 4 Translate this text into Spanish.

> Take care with agreement here.

Last summer I went to Barcelona with my friend Jenny. We like the same activities and there were lots of fun things to do. We ate too many churros! It was sunny all the time. Another time Jenny and I are going to go to the USA together.

> Use *que hacer.*

> ⭐ Look carefully at the nouns to work out the adjective agreements.

....

....

....

....

....

....

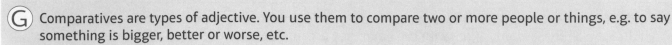

(G) Comparatives are types of adjective. You use them to compare two or more people or things, e.g. to say something is bigger, better or worse, etc.

In English, we have a number of ways to show this, including: '–er' ending (cleverer), 'more/less' (more/less interesting) and 'as … as' (as good as).

Regular comparatives

In Spanish, most comparatives are formed like this:

Spanish comparative	English meaning
más + adjective + **que**	more … than
menos + adjective + **que**	less … than
tan + adjective + **como**	as … as

In the comparative form, the adjective <u>agrees</u> with the noun being described.

*La historia es **más divertida que** la geografía.*   History is more fun than geography.
*Las ciencias son **menos creativas que** el teatro.*   Science is less creative than drama.
*Los chicos son **tan inteligentes como** las chicas.*   The boys are as intelligent as the girls.

When you compare things using verbs, the adjective is always in the masculine singular form.

*Es **más divertido** comprar en una tienda **que** comprar por Internet.*   It's more fun buying things in a shop than buying them on the internet.

Irregular comparatives

Some comparatives are irregular. They change form to agree with <u>plural</u> nouns.

singular	plural	English meaning
mejor que	mejores que	better than
peor que	peores que	worse than
mayor que	mayores que	older than
menor que	menores que	younger than

*Soy bueno en geografía pero David es **mejor que** yo.*   I'm good at geography but David is better than me.
*Mi hermana es **menor que** tu hermana.*   My sister is younger than your sister.

1 Match these sentence halves.

1 El dibujo es más
2 El inglés es tan
3 Mis deberes son
4 El francés es
5 ¿Es tu primo
6 Mi equipo es mejor

a peores que tus deberes.
b que Manchester United.
c menos interesante que el español.
d mayor que tú?
e difícil como la historia.
f interesante que la tecnología.

2 Look and choose the correct option each time.

1 Tomás es *más bajo que* / *menos bajo que* Romina.
2 Tomás es *mayor que* / *menor que* Romina.
3 Tomás es *tan gordo como* / *más gordo que* Romina.
4 Romina es *menos organizada que* / *más organizada que* Tomás.
5 Tomás es *peor que* / *mejor que* Romina en matemáticas.
6 Romina es *menos habladora que* / *tan habladora como* Tomás.

Tomás   Romina

¡Viva! GCSE Spanish © Pearson Education Limited 2017

3 Rewrite these sentences in the correct order.

1 ropa más mi uniformes que elegante es los . _____

2 tan el ciencias no es difícil español como las. _____

3 caramelos peores los son bocadillo que un . _____

4 voy pero es menos el bicicleta rápida que en autobús . _____

_____

4 Use the key to write out the following sentences in Spanish.

Key	> more than	< less than	= as … as

1 Italia es _____ (>*interesting*) Francia.

2 Unos vaqueros son _____ (<*comfortable*) unos pantalones de deporte.

3 La equitación es _____ (=*exciting*) el baloncesto.

4 Ir a pie es _____ (<*expensive*) ir en autobús.

5 Somos _____ (>*old*) nuestros primos.

6 Las clases de biología son _____ (*better*) las clases de física.

5 Write sentences in Spanish comparing each pair of items.

1 maths / languages _____

2 horror films / comedies _____

3 sport / reading _____

6 Translate these sentences into Spanish.

1 I am taller than my mother.

_____

2 Maths is less easy than PE.

_____

3 She's as shy as her brother. He is older than her.

_____

H 7 Translate this passage into Spanish.

At my school we wear a uniform. The skirt is more comfortable than a dress but the trousers are less practical than jeans. I go to school by car. It's as quick as going by bus. I love Spanish because it's better than art. I don't like science because it's not as creative as languages.

_____

_____

_____

_____

_____

_____

G You use superlatives to compare two or more things and say that one is the best, worst, clever<u>est</u>, most/least (interesting), etc.

Regular superlatives

In Spanish, most superlatives are formed like this:

el/la/los/las más + adjective	the most ...
el/la/los/las menos + adjective	the least ...

In the superlative form, the adjective <u>agrees</u> with the noun being described.

*Estos coches son **los más pequeños**.*   These cars are **the smallest**.

When the superlative is used with a noun, the noun goes <u>before</u> *más / menos*.

*La tecnología es **la asignatura menos interesante**.*   Technology is the **least** interesting subject.

Irregular superlatives

Some superlatives are irregular. They change form to agree with plural nouns and the noun goes <u>after</u> *mejor*, etc.

singular	plural	English meaning
el/la mejor	los/las mejores	the best
el/la peor	los/las peores	the worst
el/la mayor	los/las mayores	the oldest, the biggest
el/la menor	los/las menores	the youngest

*Escuché **las mejores canciones**.*   I listened to **the best songs**.

To give a context (e.g. 'the best <u>in the class</u>', 'the oldest <u>in the world</u>'), you use *de*.

*Son los mayores **de** la clase.*   They're the oldest **in** the class.

H Absolute superlatives

Use the absolute superlative when you want to say something is <u>really</u> nice or <u>extremely</u> expensive.

To form the absolute superlative, you add *–ísimo* to the end of the adjective, and make it agree.

*Es facil**ísimo**.*   It's **really** easy.

If the adjective ends in a vowel, you remove it before adding the ending.

*Estas gambas están buen**ísimas**.*   These prawns are **extremely** good.

masculine singular	feminine singular	masculine plural	feminine plural	English meaning
altísim**o**	altísim**a**	altísim**os**	altísim**as**	really/very/extremely tall

1 Complete these sentences using the words from the box.

1 La educación física es fácil: es la asignatura _____ difícil.

2 Sus amigos son los más _____ .

3 Es el campo de fútbol más _____ de España.

4 Tengo tres hermanas, pero soy la _____ .

5 No me gusta la química porque es la asignatura _____ complicada.

6 Mi profesor de dibujo es _____ mejor.

el	famoso
menos	más
mayor	divertidos

2 Unjumble the words in brackets to complete these sentences.

1 Me gusta hacer natación. Es _____ (le mjroe) deporte.

2 Javier tiene muchos amigos. Es el chico _____ (smá cibaosle) de mi grupo.

3 Gael lee mucho. Es el alumno _____ (áms letniitegne) de la clase.

4 Su profesora es paciente. Es la profe _____ (snome versea) del insti.

H 3 **Teresa Teatrera is a drama queen! Circle all the adjectives and rewrite the text for her, changing them to absolute superlatives.**

El domingo fui al (famoso) puerto de Barcelona, ¡fue divertido! Primero comí unas gambas y unas patatas bravas ricas. Luego fui a la playa, donde alquilé un barco grande, ¡era precioso! Después saqué fotos de las casas viejas del Barrio Gótico y compré dos camisetas caras en la tienda. Y ahora ¡estoy cansada!

> To keep the hard 'c' sound, *ric*– changes to *riqu*– in the absolute superlative.

El domingo fui al famosísimo puerto de Barcelona

4 **Finish these sentences with your own answers. Then translate them into English.**

En mi opinión …

1 *El deporte más emocionante es*

2 *El mejor destino de vacaciones es*

3 *La asignatura menos interesante es*

5 **Translate these sentences into Spanish.**

1 I saw the most interesting museums.

2 She wants to buy the longest necklace.

3 I am the youngest in my family.

> Remember to look carefully at verbs and use the correct tense!

> Think carefully about word order. Look back at the grammar box, if you need to.

H 6 **Translate this passage into Spanish.**

Last winter I went to New York. It was really interesting! I visited the best shops and I bought the most expensive presents. Central Park is the prettiest park in the city. On Tuesday, my sister and I went to the Metropolitan Museum where we saw the most famous paintings. It was the best holiday of my life!

> To give a context like this, use *de*.

> Singular or plural?

Quantifiers and intensifiers

» *Foundation p. 13, p. 98*
» *Higher p. 15, p. 105*

 Quantifiers are words that tell you how much (e.g. 'quite', 'enough'). **Intensifiers** are words that make the effect of an adjective stronger (e.g. 'very', 'so').

Quantifiers

These words in Spanish can be used as **adjectives** (with nouns) or as **adverbs** (with verbs or adjectives).

bastante(s)	quite, enough
demasiado(a/os/as)	too much, too many
mucho(a/os/as)	a lot
poco(a/os/as)	not much, not many, little, few
tanto(a/os/as)	so much, so many

⭐ Be careful – when using *más* or *menos* with a number use *de*, not *que*.
e.g. *Hay **más de** treinta alumnos en mi clase.*
There are **more than** thirty students in my class.

When they are adjectives, they agree with the nouns.

*Tiene **tantos** amigos.*	She has **so many** friends.
*Hay **bastante** queso.*	There's **enough** cheese.

As adverbs they do not change.

*¿Bailáis **mucho**?*	Do you dance **a lot**?
*Las botas son **demasiado** pequeñas.*	The boots are **too** small.

Intensifiers

Muy (very) and *tan* (so) are the most common intensifiers. They are adverbs – and so are used only with adjectives (very happy) and other adverbs (so slowly). They do not change.

*Estoy **muy** cansada.*	I'm **very** tired.
*¡Andas **tan** rápidamente!*	You walk **so** quickly!

1 Read and draw to match the opinion expressed: 🙂 or 🙁.

1 bastante bueno ....

2 tan emocionante ....

3 poco interesante ....

4 demasiado caro ....

5 mucho mejor ....

6 muy aburrido ....

2 Match these sentence halves.

⭐ Use your knowledge of grammar rules to work out what to match if you don't know all the words.

1 Estoy cansada porque

2 Me gusta ir a la playa porque

3 Es una ciudad bonita porque

4 Ahora no compra

5 ¡Ya has bebido

6 Hablamos muy

7 He leído más

8 ¿Cuántos necesitas?

a tantas cosas por Internet.

b bastante! ¡Para!

c hay muchos parques.

d poco francés.

e trabajo demasiado.

f es muy relajante.

g Menos de diez.

h de quince novelas este año.

H 3 Complete each sentence with the quantifier/intensifier in the correct form.

1   Llega .... (*too*) tarde.

2   Era .... (*so*) tranquilo.

3   Hay .... (*not many*) hoteles.

4   Lleva una vida .... (*quite*) frenética.

5   Hay .... (*so much*) contaminación.

6   ¿Lees .... (*a lot*) los fines de semana?

> ★ Think about whether the missing word is an adjective or an adverb. Only adjectives agree.

4 Circle the quantifiers/intensifiers. Then translate the sentences into English.

1   Los banqueros tienen demasiado dinero.

....

2   Cuando nieva, hay muy pocas razones para salir.

....

3   Los niños hambrientos no tienen suficiente comida.

....

> ★ Use what you do know and the context to work out any words you don't recognise.

5 Translate these sentences into Spanish.

1   I have so many cousins.

....

2   We don't go to the cinema much.

....

3   He ate too much food and didn't drink enough water.

....

> Adjective or adverb? Do you need to think about agreement or not?

H 6 Translate this passage into Spanish.

> Which tense do you need here?

When I was very young, I used to have a lot of friends and I did lots of activities. Now I have so little time. It's quite difficult to go out at the weekends because I have to study too much. But last Saturday I went to the theme park with my friend Ana. There were so many things to do there! It was fantastic!

....

....

....

....

....

G Adverbs are words that give more information about verbs (in the same way that adjectives give more information about nouns). They are used to say how, where and when something happens: 'I wrote this essay <u>carefully</u>'; 'He ran a marathon <u>recently</u>'; 'I <u>occasionally</u> watch that programme'. In English, they often end in '–ly'.

Many adverbs are formed from adjectives. You take the <u>feminine singular</u> form of the adjective and add the ending **–mente**:

adjective	feminine form	adverb
perfecto	perfect**a**	perfecta**mente**

Adverbs <u>do not</u> change to agree.

*Jorge canta muy **suavemente**.*   Jorge sings very softly.
*¿Ana, puedes hacerlo **inmediatamente**?*   Can you do it immediately, Ana?

The adverb form ending in **–mente** is the single most common form of Spanish adverb. However, whereas most English adverbs end in '–ly', there is a greater variety of adverb forms in Spanish (see p. 22).

1 Circle the adverbs and translate them into English.

★ The adverbs in this exercise are all cognates – use what you know to work out any that are new to you.

1 Hazlo rápidamente. ....

2 Generalmente no me gusta ir al campo. ....

3 Finalmente me lavé los dientes. ....

4 ¿Adónde vas los sábados normalmente? ....

5 Visitamos Madrid recientemente. ....

6 Desafortunadamente le duelen los pies. ....

2 Match up these word halves to make adverbs. Write them out in full and translate.

1 natural   **a** nte   ....

2 actualm   **b** e   ....

3 lentame   **c** te   ....

4 solamen   **d** mente   ....

5 clarament   **e** ente   ....

3 Make adverbs from the adjectives.

★ You don't need to move the accent on an adjective when you make it into an adverb – it stays exactly the same.

1 útil   ....   5 tímido   ....
2 abierto   ....   6 serio   ....
3 fuerte   ....   7 impaciente   ....
4 personal   ....   8 feliz   ....

4a Match these sentence halves.

1 Mi hermano *rió*

2 Corro

3 La puerta se abre

4 *Estaba leyendo*

a fácilmente con la llave.

b tranquilamente el periódico cuando llegó mi amigo.

c rápidamente para coger el autobús.

d *tontamente* cuando vio la peli.

reír – to laugh

This is from the verb *leer*. Use the rest of the sentence to work out the tense if you're not sure how to translate it.

Think carefully about how to translate this into English – 'sillily' doesn't really work. What alternatives can you come up with?

b Now translate the sentences into English.

1 ....

2 ....

3 ....

4 ....

5 Translate these sentences into Spanish.

Remember, 'fast' is an adverb in this context in English. You need to translate it into Spanish as an adverb, not an adjective.

1 Álvaro runs slowly but I run fast.

....

2 I normally arrive at 8 o'clock.

....

3 Miriam understands perfectly.

....

H 6 Translate this passage into Spanish.

Use *comportarse*.

On Saturdays I normally babysit for my neighbours' children. Generally, they behave well but sometimes they play very noisily. Luckily they love books so I read stories calmly and finally they go to sleep. Personally I would prefer to work in a shop!

Which tense do you need here?

You know the verb 'to sleep'. You'll need to make it reflexive here.

....

....

....

....

Adverbs   Adverbs of time, frequency and place

» *Foundation p. 46*
» *Higher p. 58*

G Adverbs are words that give more information about verbs (in the same way that adjectives give more information about nouns).

Many adverbs are formed from adjectives and have the ending *–mente* (see p. 20). However, there are other common adverbs and adverbial phrases that don't take this form – you just need to memorise these. Learning them in categories will help you.

adverbs of frequency ('how often')	adverbs of time ('when')	adverbs of place ('where')
cada día / todos los días (every day) **a menudo** (often) **de vez en cuando** (from time to time) **a veces** (sometimes) **una vez / dos veces … a la semana /** **al mes / al año** (once / twice … a week / a month / a year) **nunca** (never) **siempre** (always)	**ahora** (now) **ya** (already) **mañana** (tomorrow) **ayer** (yesterday) **hoy** (today) **anoche** (last night) **después** (later, then) **pronto** (soon) **temprano** (early) **tarde** (late) **más tarde** (later) **antes** (before) **mañana por la mañana / tarde** (tomorrow morning / evening) **el año que viene / el año próximo** (next year)	**aquí** (here) **ahí** (there) **allí** (over there, i.e. far away)

adverbs of manner ('how')
bien (well)   **mal** (badly)

adverbs of degree ('how much')
muy (very)   **bastante** (quite)   **demasiado** (too)   **mucho** (a lot)   **poco** (little)   **un poco** (a little)

This list is not complete. Make a note of other useful adverbs you come across when you are learning Spanish.

Some adverbs are used to intensify other adverbs and adjectives – to describe the degree to which you do something ('how much', 'how often', etc.): I wrote this essay <u>very</u> carefully. I'm <u>really</u> happy.

*Anoche fui al cine y me acosté **muy tarde**.* | **Last night** I went to the cinema and I went to bed **very late**.

*Mi padre lee un periódico **cada día** pero **nunca** ve la tele.* | My father reads a newspaper **every day** but he **never** watches TV.

---

1 **Put these adverbs of frequency in order, from the most frequent to the least frequent.**

1
cada día
dos veces al año
una vez a la semana
siempre

2
de vez en cuando
nunca
todos los días
a menudo

3
los fines de semana
cinco veces al año
cada mes
casi todos los días

1 _____ / _____ / _____ / _____

2 _____ / _____ / _____ / _____

3 _____ / _____ / _____ / _____

2 Match these sentence halves.

1 Anoche   **a** porque no quiero perder el tren.

2 ¿Qué hiciste   **b** voy a comprar una novela de ciencia ficción.

3 Mañana   **c** ya.

4 Siempre   **d** ayer?

5 Lo hemos visto   **e** leí un tebeo muy emocionante.

6 Me acuesto temprano   **f** me gusta leer los blogs.

> ⭐ Use adverbs as clues to work out which tense is required to complete the sentence.

3 Complete these sentences with the adverbs in brackets.

1 ¿Lo hace _____ (*well*)?

2 Le llamo _____ (*soon*) y _____ (*then*) salgo.

3 Vio a los hombres _____ (*over there*).

4 _____ (*Yesterday*) fuimos al cine y _____ (*tomorrow morning*) vamos a la playa.

5 Cantan muy _____ (*badly*).

4 Circle the correct option and translate the sentence(s) into English.

1 Ayer *visito / visité / voy a visitar* el zoo.

    ....

2 No quiero salir de casa ahora. ¿Por qué no vienes tú *aquí / ahí / allí*?

    ....

3 No me gusta nada hacer deporte, es *mucho / demasiado / poco* aburrido.

    ....

4 Me chifla mandar SMS, ¡estoy enganchado! Lo hago *de vez en cuando / nunca / cada día*.

    ....

> Think about the sense of the opinion expressed to help you work out which word to select.

5 Translate these sentences into Spanish.

1 I always watch that programme. ....

2 Tomorrow I'm going to go to school early.

    ....

3 You speak Spanish really well.

    ....

> Which tense do you need to use here?

> You need to use two adverbs here – make sure you put them in the correct order!

Ⓗ 6 Translate this passage into Spanish.

Happy New Year! This year I'm going to be better. I'm not going to surf the net every day and my friend and I are going to play tennis twice a week. Last year I didn't always do my homework very well, but from now I'm going to study a lot. I need to go to bed early every night and only watch TV from time to time.

> Which word do you need here? Look at comparatives on p. 14 if you need a reminder.

> Take care with the negative here.

....

....

....

....

Interrogatives Asking questions

» *Foundation p. 35, p. 93*
» *Higher p. 39, p. 99*

G There are two ways to ask a question in Spanish:

- For a yes/no answer, you use the sentence structure with a questioning (rising) intonation.

  ¿Hablas español?   Do you speak Spanish?

- For open-ended questions, you use question words. These always come at the start of the question and have an accent.

question word	English meaning
cuál(es)	which
cuánto/a/os/as	how much/how many
cómo	how
dónde (adónde)	where
qué	what
quién	who
a qué hora	at what time

⭐ In Spanish, all questions have punctuation at the start and end.

Question words fall into three categories: interrogative adjectives, adverbs and pronouns.

Interrogative adjectives

Interrogative adjectives are followed by nouns. *Cuál* and *cuánto* need to agree with the noun in number and gender. *Qué* is invariable (it does not change).

  *¿**Cuántos** libros tienes?*   **How many** books do you have?
  *¿**Qué** deportes haces?*   **What** sports do you do?

Interrogative adverbs

Interrogative adverbs are usually followed by a verb.

  *¿**Dónde** vives?*   **Where** do you live?   *¿**Adónde** vamos?*   Where are we going?
  *¿**Por qué** no comes carne?*   **Why** don't you eat meat?   *¿**Cuánto** cuestan?*   How much do they cost?

Interrogative pronouns

Interrogative pronouns are question words that replace nouns.

  *¿**Cuáles** son tus asignaturas preferidas?*   **Which (ones)** are your favourite subjects?

1 Find and match the words and meanings.

quéadóndequiéncómodóndecuántoscuálporquécuándoaquéhora

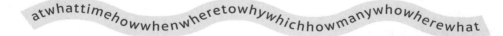

atwhattimehowwhenwheretowhywhichhowmanywhowherewhat

2 Match the phrases in the first and second columns to form a question, then find the answer to the question in the third column.

1	¿Qué	a	fuiste de vacaciones?	i	En la calle Mayor.
2	¿Dónde	b	vamos a llegar?	ii	Francia.
3	¿Cuántos	c	años tiene Luz?	iii	Es hablador.
4	¿Cómo	d	te gusta hacer?	iv	Natación.
5	¿Adónde	e	vives?	v	A las ocho.
6	¿Cuándo	f	es tu mejor amigo?	vi	Quince años.

¡Viva! GCSE Spanish © Pearson Education Limited 2017

H 3 Using the right question word and any other words you need, write out the full questions in Spanish.

1 ¿... tu color favorito?

_____

2 ¿... tu cantante favorita?

_____

3 ¿... tu cumpleaños?

_____

4 ¿... desayunas por la mañana?

_____

5 ¿... lo mejor de tu visita?

_____

_____

4 Complete these questions with the correct question word, then translate the questions and answers into English.

1 ¿ _____ va al insti? A las siete.

_____

2 ¿ _____ te preparas? Me aliso el pelo.

_____

3 ¿ _____ prefieres el tren? Es más rápido.

_____

4 ¿ _____ alumnos hay en la clase? Treinta.

_____

5 Translate these sentences into Spanish.

> Remember – you don't translate 'do' into Spanish.

> ⭐ Remember to use Spanish question punctuation – and don't forget the accents on question words.

1 When do you play tennis?

_____

2 What do you do in your free time?

_____

3 Where is the park?

_____

H 6 Translate this passage into Spanish.

> What kind of question is this – yes/no or open?

> Don't panic when you see a negative! The same rules apply – question word at the start, negative before or around the verb.

How are you, Luna? Are you going to go to Gael's house on Friday? Why is your boyfriend not going to come? What time does it start? What are you going to bring? Did you buy some cakes? How many cakes? Where did you buy them? See you later!

_____

_____

_____

_____

Pronouns Subject pronouns

» Foundation p. 15
» Higher p. 17

(G) Pronouns are used in place of nouns, for example, 'I', 'you', 'it', 'them', etc. and fall into two categories: **subject pronouns** and **object pronouns** (for object pronouns, see p. 32).

singular subject pronouns		plural subject pronouns	
yo	I	*nosotros/nosotras*	we
tú	you (informal singular)	*vosotros/vosotras*	you (informal plural)
él	he/it	*ellos*	they (masculine)
ella	she/it	*ellas*	they (feminine)
usted	you (formal singular)	*ustedes*	you (formal plural)

In English, subject pronouns are used with verbs all of the time ('**I** go', '**we** are watching', etc.). But often you don't need to use them in Spanish – the verb form (usually the ending) makes it clear who is being referred to: *voy* – I go, *van* – they go; *viajo* – I travel, *viajamos* – we travel. Subject pronouns are generally only used for emphasis or clarity in Spanish.

> ⭐ Watch out for accents: *él* means 'he/it' but *el* means 'the'. Don't mix them up!

*¿Y **tú**, qué opinas?*	What do **you** think?
***Yo** estudio ciencias pero **él** estudia teatro.*	**I** study science but **he** studies drama.

Usted and ustedes

For 'you', as well as having different forms for singular and plural, Spanish also distinguishes between formal (polite) and informal use. With people you know well, you use *tú* and *vosotros/vosotras*. In a more formal situation, you should use *usted* (+ 'he/she/it' form of the verb) or *ustedes* (+ 'they' form of the verb). Again, the pronouns are sometimes left out.

*¿Qué **va** a tomar (**usted**)?*	What are **you** going to have?	*¿De dónde **son** (**ustedes**)?*	Where are **you (plural)** from?

1 Choose the correct subject pronoun each time.

1 *Él / Ella* es trabajador.

2 ¿Señora López, qué quiere *tú / usted*?

3 Los alumnos van a la piscina pero *nosotros / ellas* vamos al comedor.

4 *Tú / Usted* no puedes venir conmigo.

5 Tú vas a llegar a las ocho pero *yo / ustedes* voy a llegar tarde.

6 *Ellos / Vosotros* no hablan francés.

2 Write the correct subject pronoun(s) for each verb.

1 _____ habláis

2 _____ acampamos

3 _____ fue

4 _____ hago

5 _____ vuelven

6 _____ puedes

3 Circle the subject pronoun in each sentence, then translate the sentences into English.

1 ¿Y tú, qué quieres hacer? _____

2 Ella y yo estamos felices. _____

3 ¿Ustedes pueden recomendarme un libro? _____

4 Translate these sentences into Spanish using the correct subject pronouns.

> ⭐ Remember to double-check you are using the correct form of the verb each time.

1 Mr Gómez, you (polite) can't go out. _____

2 He wants to dance but I want to have dinner. _____

3 Jorge, where are you? We're in the café. _____

Pronouns Reflexive pronouns

Foundation p. 111
Higher p. 62, p. 117

G There is one instance in which you always see pronouns with verbs. Reflexive verbs, which are often used to talk about daily routines, opinions, emotions and relationships, contain a pronoun <u>before</u> the verb.

me	myself	*nos*	ourselves
te	yourself (informal singular)	*os*	yourselves (informal plural)
se	himself/herself/itself/oneself/ yourself (formal singular)	*se*	themselves, yourselves (formal plural)

The pronoun is not usually translated in English.

Me *levanto a las ocho.* I get up at eight.
Se *lleva bien con sus padres.* He gets on well with his parents.

In the infinitive form, the pronoun comes at the end of the verb.

*Suele acostar**se** a las diez.* She usually goes to bed at 10.

Other uses of the reflexive pronoun

Other verbs use reflexive pronouns for shared actions between two or more people. These are plural forms and mean 'each other'.

Nos conocemos *desde hace cinco años.* We have known **each other** for five years.
Se apoyan *en todo.* They support **each other** in everything.

1 Complete the verb with the correct reflexive pronouns.

_____ llamo   _____ llamamos
_____ llamas   _____ llamáis
_____ llama   _____ llaman

2 Correct the reflexive pronoun in each sentence.

1 Se llamo Ana. _____

2 Javier os despierta a las seis. _____

3 Desayunan después de ducharme. _____

4 Mis padres y yo os llevamos muy bien. _____

5 ¿Nos peinas, Ana? _____

6 Se laváis los dientes. _____

3 Translate these sentences into English.

> The pronoun is often not translated directly in English.

1 Nos despertamos y nos vestimos. _____

2 Me baño y después me acuesto. _____

3 Jorge se lava la cara pero no se ducha. _____

4 Translate these sentences into Spanish.

1 I wash my hair every day.

_____

2 He has a shower.

_____

3 We have breakfast at school.

_____

⭐ Remember to check that the pronoun and verb ending match.

Remember when you're translating, you don't always translate word for word. In Spanish you can use a single verb for 'to have a shower'.

H 4 I can't get up straightaway.

_____

¡Viva! GCSE Spanish © Pearson Education Limited 2017

27

Pronouns Emphatic pronouns

G Pronouns are used in place of a noun, to avoid repeating it. Emphatic pronouns are used after prepositions and in other situations to <u>emphasise</u> the noun they replace. With the exception of *mí*, *ti* and *sí*, they are the same as the equivalent subject pronouns.

Make sure the pronoun agrees with the noun it replaces!

singular		plural	
mí	me	*nosotros / nosotras*	us
ti	you	*vosotros / vosotras*	you (plural)
él	him	*ellos*	them (m)
ella	her	*ellas*	them (f)
usted	you (polite singular)	*ustedes*	you (polite plural)
sí	himself / herself / yourself	*sí*	themselves / yourselves

*Voy sin **ti**.*	I'm going without **you**.
*¿Son para **nosotros**?*	Are they for **us**?
*A **mí** no me gusta el pollo.*	**I** don't like chicken.

When the preposition *con* ('with') is used with *mí*, *ti* or *sí*, it merges with the pronoun to create a single form: ***conmigo**, **contigo**, **consigo**.*

*Trabajó **conmigo**.*   He worked **with me**.

⭐ To emphasise that you like or dislike something with *gustar*, you need to use the word *a* before *mí*, just as you would when you talk about what someone else likes (e.g. *A **Laura** le gusta nadar*). *A* is a preposition, so it is followed by the emphatic pronoun: '*A **mí** …*' (literally 'To me …').

1 Match these Spanish and English phrases.

1 delante de él
2 para mí
3 contigo
4 al lado de usted
5 enfrente de ella
6 detrás de vosotras

a beside you (polite)
b opposite her
c for me
d in front of him
e with you
f behind you (plural)

⭐ Use the prepositions and the pronouns to help you work out the matching pairs.

H 2 Complete these sentences with the prepositions and pronouns in brackets.

1 Tengo un regalo ——————. (*for you, polite singular*)

2 En la foto, Javier está ——————. (*behind us, feminine*)

3 ¿Los chicos? Vamos a ir ——————. (*without them, masculine*)

4 —————— les gustan los Estados Unidos. (*You, polite plural*)

5 Ellos hablan ——————. (*about me*)

6 Lo trajo ——————. (*with him*)

Remember that *con* merges with some pronouns to create a single word.

3 Translate these sentences into Spanish.

1 He has something for you.

2 He really likes sport but I don't like sport at all.

3 Do you want to dance with me?

Remember to use the emphatic pronouns to emphasise the contrast between the two subjects.

H 4 In my opinion, the biggest problem is hunger.

Which preposition and pronoun can you use to translate this?

¡Viva! GCSE Spanish © Pearson Education Limited 2017

Pronouns Possessive pronouns

(G) Possessive pronouns are words like 'mine', 'yours', 'hers', 'theirs'. They are used in place of nouns that show possession: 'It's ~~my book~~.' → 'It's <u>mine</u>.' In Spanish the pronoun agrees in gender and number with the noun it is replacing (not with the person who is the owner).

Note that you use the same forms for 'his / hers' (etc.) and 'theirs'.

singular		plural		English meaning
masculine	feminine	masculine	feminine	
el mío	la mía	los míos	las mías	mine
el tuyo	la tuya	los tuyos	las tuyas	yours (singular)
el suyo	la suya	los suyos	las suyas	his, hers, its, yours (polite)
el nuestro	la nuestra	los nuestros	las nuestras	ours
el vuestro	la vuestra	los vuestros	las vuestras	yours (plural)
el suyo	la suya	los suyos	las suyas	theirs, yours (plural)

*Mi libro es interesante. ¿Y **el tuyo**?*   My book is interesting. And **yours**?

*Nuestro insti es más grande que **el vuestro**.*   Our school is bigger than **yours**.

You don't usually use the definite article with the possessive pronoun when it comes <u>after</u> the verb *ser*.

*Ese libro **es mío**.*   That book **is mine**.

1 Circle the correct forms.

1 Tu móvil es más nuevo que *el mío / la mía*.

2 Me gustan sus pantalones. *Los míos / Las mías* son feos.

3 Mi casa es moderna pero *el suyo / la suya* es antigua.

4 Estas revistas son muy interesantes. ¿Son *tuyos / tuyas*?

5 Ese insti es enorme. *El nuestro / la nuestra* es muy pequeño.

(H) 2 Complete these sentences with the correct possessive pronouns.

> ⭐ Look carefully at the verb to work out the owner each time. But remember: the pronoun agrees with the noun it is replacing – not the owner.

1 Es mi móvil. Es _____ .

2 Compramos estos caramelos. Son _____ .

3 Tienes una gorra nueva. _____ es más bonita que la mía.

4 Ben perdió unos lápices, pero no son aquellos. _____ son azules.

5 Si tus auriculares están rotos, ¿quieres usar _____ ? Yo no los necesito.

(H) 3 Translate these sentences into Spanish.

> Should this agree with 'Lucy' or 'boots'?

1 Lucy, these boots are yours. _____

> Use *la mochila*.

2 The blue suitcase is mine and the red backpack is his. _____

_____

3 Which team won on Saturday, ours or theirs? _____

4 I've forgotten my calculator. Can I use yours? _____

Pronouns Relative pronouns

G You use relative pronouns – in English, 'who', 'whom', 'which' and 'that' – to introduce more information about the noun (the person or thing) you are talking about. We don't always include the relative pronoun in English, but you must include it in Spanish. The main relative pronouns in Spanish are *que* and *quien(es)*.

Que

The relative pronoun *que* ('who', 'whom', 'which', 'that') can refer to a person or thing.

   *La mujer **que** ves en la foto es mi tía.*   The woman (whom) you see in the photo is my aunt.

If you use *que* after a preposition, you must include the article with the pronoun: *el que*, *la que*, *los que*, *las que*.

   *La casa **en la que** vivimos es grande.*   The house **in which** we live is big.

If *el que* is used with *a* or *de*, the preposition and article combine: *al que*, *del que*.

Lo que

You use the relative pronoun *lo que* to refer to the previous part of a sentence or to introduce a general idea.

   *Hay riesgo de tormentas, **lo que** me asusta.*   There's a risk of storms, **which** scares me.
   ***Lo que** más me gustó fue la comida.*   **What** I liked most was the food.

Quien(es)

Quien(es) ('who', 'whom') can only refer to a person or people. It must agree in number with the noun it refers to: use *quien* for one person and *quienes* for more than one person.

   *Las chicas con **quienes** hablamos fueron divertidas.*   The girls (whom) we talked to were fun.

H ### Cuyo

You use the relative pronoun *cuyo* ('whose') to show possession. It must agree in gender and in number with the noun it replaces, <u>not</u> the owner: *cuyo*, *cuya*, *cuyos*, *cuyas*.

   *El equipo, **cuya** mascota es un perro, ganó.*   The team, whose mascot is a dog, won.

---

1 **Circle the relative pronoun. Then translate the sentences into English.**

  1 Hablé con el chico que viene aquí todos los días.

     _____

  2 Esas son las chicas con quienes trabajo.

     _____

  3 El vestido que compró ayer costó mucho dinero.

     _____

  4 La tienda a la que siempre vamos está cerrada.

     _____

H **2** **Cross out and correct the errors in these sentences.**

  1 ¿Cómo se llaman las mujeres con quien trabajas? _____

  2 La película de que siempre habla fue muy aburrida. _____

  3 El parque a el que vamos los domingos es bonito. _____

  4 No se lleva bien con sus padres, que es bastante triste. _____

3 **Translate these sentences into Spanish.**

  1 That man, who always wears yellow shoes, is good-looking.

     _____

  2 The coat that I want to buy is black.

     _____

H **3** The school that I go to is near here.

     _____

> Don't forget to include *a* for 'to'. Which form of the pronoun do you use with a preposition?

Pronouns Interrogative pronouns

G You use interrogative pronouns – 'who?', 'whose?', 'which?', and 'what?' – to replace a noun when asking questions. *Cuál* and *quién* must agree in number with the noun they replace.

singular	plural	English meaning
¿Qué?	¿Qué?	What?
¿Cuál?	¿Cuáles?	Which?
¿Quién?	¿Quiénes?	Who?

*¿**Qué** quieres decir con eso?*   What do you mean by that?
*¿**Cuáles** son los tuyos?*   Which (ones) are yours?
*¿**Quién** ganó?*   Who won?

1 Choose the correct interrogative pronoun to complete each sentence.

1 *¿Qué / Quién* quieres beber?

2 *¿Cuál / Cuáles* son los alumnos más listos?

3 *¿A quiénes / qué* les gusta tocar el piano?

4 Tengo dos cuadernos. *¿Cuál / Quién* es el cuaderno de Ana?

2 Complete these sentences with the correct interrogative pronoun(s).

1 ¿............... quieres ver en el cine?

2 ¿Te gustan los dos coches? ¿............... te gusta más?

3 Vamos a ir a Salamanca mañana. ¿............... van a ir en coche y .... van a ir en autobús?

4 ¿............... va a la piscina mañana a las ocho?

5 Los bolsos pequeños o los bolsos grandes, ¿............... son los mejores?

3 Translate these sentences into Spanish.

1 I like this painting. Which one do you like?

> Singular or plural? Look carefully at the first sentence.

....

2 What is he doing?

....

3 Who are those women?

> Singular or plural? Look carefully at the verb.

....

H 4 Translate this passage into Spanish.

> Singular or plural?

It's going to be very exciting on Saturday! I'm going to bring a cake. Which would you like – a strawberry cake or a chocolate cake? And some drinks? Which do you prefer? Who's going to come? What are we going to do on the beach? Are we going to do any water sports? Which ones?

> Remember, if it is a yes or no question, in Spanish it is written as a statement with question marks: Is he coming? *¿Viene?*

....

....

....

....

....

(G) There are two kinds of object pronouns: **direct** and **indirect**. They replace something or someone that has already been mentioned.

Direct object pronouns replace nouns that are directly affected by the action of the verb, i.e. they have the action done directly to them: *Marta ate ~~the cake~~ it.*

singular direct object pronouns		plural direct object pronouns	
me	me	*nos*	us
te	you (informal singular)	*os*	you (informal plural)
lo	him/it/you (formal singular masculine)	*los*	them (masculine)/you (formal plural masculine)
la	her/it/you (formal singular feminine)	*las*	them (feminine)/you (formal plural feminine)

Direct object pronouns usually go directly <u>before</u> the verb, and <u>after</u> a negative word..

*¿La leche? No **la** bebo nunca.*　　Milk? I never drink **it**.
*No **lo** quiero.*　　I don't want it.

You use the direct object pronoun to replace nouns when using verbs with the personal *a* (see p. 89).

*Vi **a** Ana. **La** vi ayer.*　　I saw Ana. I saw **her** yesterday.

In verb forms with the infinitive the pronoun can also go at the end of the infinitive.

*Puedo hacer**lo**.*　　I can do **it**.　　*Voy a llevar**los**.*　　I am going to wear **them**.

The direct object pronoun is also added to the end of an imperative.

*¡Hága**lo** así!*　　Do **it** like this!

> ★ Look at the noun each time. You need to work out the gender to find the correct pronoun.

1 **Choose the correct direct object pronoun to complete each sentence.**

1　Toco la trompeta. *Lo / La* toco.
2　Participé en un concurso. *Lo / La* gané.
3　Me chiflan las uvas. *Los / Las* como cada día.
4　Mira sus zapatos. *Los / Las* lleva todos los días.
5　Mi madre *nos / os* ayuda en casa con los deberes.
6　Carlos, no *te / me* vi en el museo.

(H) **2** **Complete each sentence with the correct direct object pronoun for the noun in brackets.**

1　_____ hago por la tarde. (*los deberes*)
2　_____ visitó en el hospital. (*tú*)
3　_____ odio. (*el té*)
4　_____ saqué. (*las fotos*)
5　¿Puedes mandar _____? (*un SMS*)
6　No quiere llevar _____ porque es fea. (*camisa*)

3 **Circle the correct noun, then translate these sentences into English.**

1　Jorge la tiene. *libro / pelota* _____

2　Los compramos en el mercado. *pasteles / patatas* _____

3　Las vi ayer. *amigos / chicas* _____

> Do you need *lo* or *la* here for 'it'?

(H) **4** **Translate these sentences into Spanish.**

1　I play the guitar. I play it every day. _____

2　Where is my phone? I don't have it. _____

3　I bought some magazines. I'm going to read them tomorrow.

_____

¡Viva! GCSE Spanish © Pearson Education Limited 2017

Pronouns Indirect object pronouns

>> Higher p. 146

(G) Indirect object pronouns replace nouns that are indirectly affected by the action of the verb, i.e. they have the action done indirectly to them: 'Luis gave the cake to ~~Marta~~ her.'

Note that in English the word 'to' or 'for' is often omitted: 'Luis gave her the cake.'

Indirect object pronouns normally answer the question, 'to whom?' or 'for whom?'

singular		plural	
me	(to/for) me	**nos**	(to/for) us
te	(to/for) you (informal singular)	**os**	(to/for) you (informal plural)
le	(to/for) him/her/it/you (formal singular)	**les**	(to/for) them/you (formal plural)

Indirect object pronouns usually go <u>before</u> the verb.

Me apetece trabajar en España.   Working in Spain appeals **to me**.
*Ayer vi a Nuria y **le** di el libro.*   I saw Nuria yesterday and I gave **her** the book.

In verb forms with the infinitive (e.g. with *querer* or in the near future tense), the indirect object pronoun can also go at the end of the infinitive.

Te voy a escribir. / Voy a escribirte.   I am going to write **to you**.

1 Find the indirect object pronoun and translate it into English.

1 Javier me mandó un SMS. _____

2 El padre les compra un regalo. _____

3 ¿Puedes darle tu dirección? _____

4 Quiero decirte algo. _____

5 Les dijimos adiós. _____

6 Mi madre nos prepara la cena. _____

> Remember, the pronoun comes <u>before</u> the verb – so look for the verbs to help you recognise the pronouns.

(H) 2 Rewrite these sentences, incorporating the correct indirect object pronoun in the correct position.

> Where does the pronoun go – before or after the verb?

1 David trae los DVD. (to me) _____

2 Compraron un collar. (for you, singular) _____

3 Quiero dar unos tebeos. (to them) _____

4 Ben escribe una carta. (to us) _____

5 Penélope no habla. (to you, plural) _____

(H) 3 Translate these sentences into Spanish.

1 I buy her a book.

2 He sends us some flowers.

3 My cousins like to go to the cinema. I sent them a DVD.

4 They talk to you (informal plural) often.

5 Ana and I want to go to the beach and so I'm going to give her some sunglasses.

> 'Her' looks like a direct object pronoun – but it's really 'for her'. Remember, we don't always use 'to/for' in English in this context.

> Pronoun before or after the verb? The fact that the verb is in the preterite doesn't make any difference.

> Where can you put the pronoun when the verb structure uses an infinitive?

Pronouns Demonstrative pronouns

» *Foundation p. 96*
» *Higher p. 102*

(G) Demonstrative pronouns are used to indicate a particular thing: 'this one', 'that one', 'that one over there'. These words <u>agree in gender and number</u> with the noun they replace. The masculine and feminine forms are the same as the demonstrative adjectives.

singular			plural		English meaning
masculine	**feminine**	**neuter**	**masculine**	**feminine**	
est**e**	est**a**	est**o**	est**os**	est**as**	this (one), these (ones)
es**e**	es**a**	es**o**	es**os**	es**as**	that (one), those (ones)
aqu**el**	aqu**ella**	aqu**ello**	aqu**ellos**	aqu**ellas**	that (one) / those (ones) over there

¿Qué gorra te gusta?   *¿Esta, esa o aquella?*
Which cap do you like?   **This one**, **that one** or **that one over there**?

Note there is also a neuter form. You use this to talk about something you don't recognise or about an idea.

¿Qué es **esto**?   What's this?   *Eso* es mentira.   That is not true.

You may see demonstrative pronouns with accents (e.g. *éste, aquéllos*), as they were written like this in the past. This doesn't change their meaning, but it is no longer the recommended form.

1 **Match each noun to the correct pronoun and the correct translation.**

el abrigo	esa	these
la tienda	estos	that one over there
las fotos	aquel	those over there
los libros	aquellas	that one

(H) **2** **Complete with the correct demonstrative pronoun.**

1 cuadro (*this one*) _____
2 flores (*those over there*) _____
3 árboles (*those*) _____

4 botellas (*these*) _____
5 pastel (*that one over there*) _____
6 sudadera (*that one*) _____

3 **Translate these sentences into Spanish.**

1 I don't want this pen – I want that one.

_____

2 I like sweets. Can I eat those ones over there?

_____

> Remember, you only need one word for this. Which demonstrative pronoun do you need?

3 This is good.

_____

(H) **4** **Translate this passage into Spanish.**

– I want a pair of black jeans. What do you think of those?
– These ones?
– No – the ones over there.
– They're quite nice. But what's that? It's really ugly!
– It's a really cool T-shirt! I'm going to buy it. I tried on that one but I prefer this one.

> In Spanish you use 'some' for this.

> Near to or far from the person?

> You could use the absolute superlative here.

_____
_____
_____

Pronouns Indefinite pronouns

G Indefinite pronouns are used to talk about something or someone unspecific, or to refer to things or people in a general way: 'something', 'no one', 'anyone'.

algo	something, anything	**alguien**	someone, anyone
nada	nothing, anything (with negative)	**nadie**	no one, anyone (with negative)

¿Tiene **algo** para el dolor de cabeza?	Do you have **anything** for a headache?
¿**Alguien** puede ayudarme?	Can **anyone** help me?
No vi a **nadie**.	I didn't see **anyone**.
No compramos **nada**.	We didn't buy **anything**.

1 Circle the correct word to complete each sentence.

1 Tengo *algo / nadie* para ti.

2 ¿Me llamó *nada / alguien*?

3 ¿Quieres tomar *nadie / algo*?

4 No tiene *nada / algo*.

5 Necesito que *alguien / nada* me ayude.

6 No conozco a *nadie / alguien*.

> ⭐ Spanish uses a double negative in sentences like the one in question 4, so it's 'He doesn't have nothing', not 'He doesn't have anything'.

2 Match these sentence halves. Then translate the sentences into English.

1 ¿Me puedes dar

2 Alguien

3 Siempre hay algo

4 No voy a comprar

5 No conozco

6 Un buen amigo es

a a nadie aquí. ....

b alguien que te hace reír. ....

c le ha visto. ....

d que hacer. ....

e algo de comer? ....

f nada por Internet. ....

3 Translate these sentences into Spanish.

> Remember to use the personal *a* with people.

1 He doesn't help anyone. ....

2 I can see something green. ....

3 Do you want anything else? Nothing else, thanks. ....

H 4 Translate this passage into Spanish.

> Use *que* + the infinitive here.

I'm a journalist. I love my job. The best thing is that there's always something to do. I write for lots of magazines. There is no one as hard-working as me! If I have nothing to sort out in the office, I interview people in their houses. A good journalist is someone who is curious and responsible.

> Spanish uses 'I' here.

> Which verb could you use here?

....

....

....

....

....

(G) Verbs are used in different tenses. Tenses tell us when the action of the verb happened, is happening or will happen, i.e. in the past, present or future.

You use the **present tense** to talk about things that are taking place now or happen repeatedly or are general statements of fact or belief.

> *Lleva* una camiseta.   She's wearing a T-shirt.   *Vivo* en Madrid.   I live in Madrid.

It is also used for things that you are planning to do soon.

> *¿Me mandas un SMS luego?*   Will you send me a text later?

In Spanish, the ending of the verb tells you who or what the subject is. There are two types of verb: regular and irregular. **Regular verbs** have the same pattern of endings. **Irregular verbs** don't follow these patterns and have to be learned individually (see pp. 38–39).

Categories of regular verb

In Spanish, regular verbs fall into three categories. You can identify them by the **infinitive** form (the form used in the dictionary which does not express any particular tense or person): the different groups end in *–ar*, *–er* and *–ir*. To make the different forms, remove *–ar*, *–er* or *–ir* to find the stem (the part that does not change). Then add the following endings to the stem.

	hab**lar** (to speak)	com**er** (to eat)	escrib**ir** (to write)
(yo)	habl**o**	com**o**	escrib**o**
(tú)	habl**as**	com**es**	escrib**es**
(él/ella/usted)	habl**a**	com**e**	escrib**e**
(nosotros/nosotras)	habl**amos**	com**emos**	escrib**imos**
(vosotros/vosotras)	habl**áis**	com**éis**	escrib**ís**
(ellos/ellas/ustedes)	habl**an**	com**en**	escrib**en**

Exceptions

Some verbs are regular in the present tense apart from the 'I' form: *hago* (*hacer* – to do/make), *salgo* (*salir* – to go out), *veo* (*ver* – to see/watch).

Key time expressions

To help you recognise the present tense, look out for key time expressions like these: *hoy* (today), *ahora* (now), *en este momento* (now), *los lunes* (on Mondays), *todos los días* (every day).

1 **Circle the correct verb form. Then translate the verbs into English.**

> ⭐ Look carefully at the ending to help you identify the correct verb form.

1 tú   *entras / entramos*   ....

2 él   *escucho / escucha*   ....

3 nosotras   *salís / salimos*   ....

4 ellas   *ven / ves*   ....

5 yo   *hago / hace*   ....

6 vosotros   *vivo / vivís*   ....

2 **Look at the infinitives and highlight the stem of each verb. Then complete the sentence with the correct form.**

1 trabajar   Yo .... como voluntario.

2 leer   Señor Gómez, ¿usted .... novelas?

3 tocar   Los chicos .... el saxofón.

4 correr   Ana .... más rápido que yo.

5 compartir   Mis padres y yo .... una pizza.

6 ayudar   ¿............................. a tu madre?

H 3 Identify and correct the errors in the verbs.

⭐ Identify the infinitive form – then you will know which endings to use.

1 Mis amigos y yo toca el teclado dos veces a la semana. ....

2 Jorge abramos la ventana. ....

3 Cuando sus tías viajáis por España, siempre compras recuerdos. ....

4 ¿Isabel y Juan, no bebes limonada? ....

5 ¿Dónde vive tus primos? ....

6 Cuando hace calor, yo nadan pero mi amigo descansas. ....

4 Look at the verb table on page 36. What patterns can you find in the endings across the three categories to help you translate the verbs correctly?

1 *yo* form: ....

2 *él/ella/usted* form: ....

3 *nosotros/nosotras* form: ....

4 *vosotros/vosotras* form: ....

5 *–ar* verbs: ....

6 *–er* verbs: ....

5 Translate these sentences into Spanish.

Look very carefully at the subject of each verb in a sentence – it isn't always the same for each one.

1 We live in the country but our mother works in the city.

....

2 I don't drink milk and my brother doesn't eat cheese.

....

3 Ana sees Luke every day. They read books in the library.

....

H 6 Translate this passage into Spanish.

Use *encargar*.

At the weekends, I work in a bookshop with a café. All the shop assistants speak lots of languages. We sell books and we also help the customers. My manager looks for and orders books online. In the afternoon, I prepare drinks in the café. Where do you work? Do you and your friends earn a lot of money?

....

....

....

....

Verbs The present tense: irregular verbs

» *Foundation p. 8*
» *Higher p. 8, p. 11*

(G) Regular verbs have a set pattern of endings in the present tense (see pp. 36–37), but irregular verbs do not follow these patterns and have to be learned individually. The verbs you will use most frequently in Spanish are all irregular – so you need to learn them thoroughly and practise them often. The table below gives the present tense for four of the most common irregular verbs.

	ser (to be)	estar (to be)	ir (to go)	tener (to have)
(yo)	soy	estoy	voy	tengo
(tú)	eres	estás	vas	tienes
(él/ella/usted)	es	está	va	tiene
(nosotros/nosotras)	somos	estamos	vamos	tenemos
(vosotros/vosotras)	sois	estáis	vais	tenéis
(ellos/ellas/ustedes)	son	están	van	tienen

Some verbs are regular in the present tense apart from the 'I' form:

hago (*hacer* – to do/make) *salgo* (*salir* – to go out) *veo* (*ver* – to see/watch)
conozco (*conocer* – to know) *sé* (*saber* – to know) *pongo* (*poner* – to put)
doy (*dar* – to give) *traigo* (*traer* – to bring)

Ser and *estar*

Note that there are two verbs for 'to be' in Spanish: *ser* and *estar*. See p. 42 for full details on when to use them. To complete the activities in this section, bear in mind that you use:

• *ser* for descriptions/characteristics and times
• *estar* for location, feelings and states of being.

---

1 Connect each verb to its meaning in English and the correct infinitive.

1 voy	a they are			
2 están	b I go	ir		
3 tengo	c I am			
4 está	d he is	estar		
5 van	e we are			
6 tiene	f they go	ser		
7 somos	g I have			
8 soy	h she has	tener		

2 Complete this grid with the correct verb forms. Can you see any patterns that might help you remember the different forms?

subject	tener	ir	estar	ser
Ana			está	
Ana and José	tienen			
Ana and I				somos
I		voy		

¡Viva! GCSE Spanish © Pearson Education Limited 2017

3 Complete these sentences with the correct form(s) of the correct irregular verb(s): *ser, estar, ir* or *tener*.

1 Mi hermano _____ gordito. En esta foto _____ un poco triste.

> Think: is *triste* a description/characteristic or a way you might feel? What about *gordito*?

2 ¿Qué día _____ biología, Belén? Yo _____ química los lunes.

3 De vez en cuando mis amigos y yo _____ de paseo.

> You can't have two present tense verbs in a row. What form of the verb do you need after *querer*?

4 Jorge, ¿cómo _____ al insti por la mañana? Yo _____ en coche.

5 No quiero _____ al cine. ¿_____ cansado? ¡No, _____ perezoso!

6 ¿Qué hora _____? _____ las tres.

4 Match these sentences halves. Then translate the sentences into English.

1 ¿De dónde   a hago mucho deporte.   _____

2 Tú   b está contento?   _____

3 Yo   c tiene hermanos.   _____

4 Es hijo único: no d eres hablador.   _____

5 ¿Su primo   e son ustedes?   _____

5 Translate these sentences into Spanish.

1 The girls are tall and they have freckles.

_____

2 My best friend goes to school by bus but I go on foot.

_____

3 I'm Ana. I'm fifteen years old. I'm in Madrid.

> Remember, you don't use *ser* or *estar* to give your age. Which verb do you use?

_____

> Ser or estar for location?

6 Translate this passage into Spanish.

My friend Greig is Scottish. He has a sister and two brothers. He goes to my school but his flat is far away. He's very cool! I know his brothers. I like them because they're really amusing but I know they are sometimes silly, too. Normally Greig and I are too tired to play with them. What are your friends like?

> Remember there are two verbs for 'to know' – *saber* and *conocer*. Which do you need here?

> Ser or estar for how you are feeling?

_____

_____

_____

_____

(G) Some verbs in the present tense have a spelling change in the stem (the stem is the part of the verb that you add the endings to). There are three main kinds of stem-changing verbs, those where the **e** in the infinitive changes to **ie**; those where the **o** changes to **ue**; and those where the **e** changes to **i**.

	e → ie pensar (to think)	o → ue poder (to be able to/can)	e → i pedir (to ask for)
(yo)	p**ie**nso	p**ue**do	p**i**do
(tú)	p**ie**nsas	p**ue**des	p**i**des
(él/ella/usted)	p**ie**nsa	p**ue**de	p**i**de
(nosotros/nosotras)	pensamos	podemos	pedimos
(vosotros/vosotras)	pensáis	podéis	pedís
(ellos/ellas/ustedes)	p**ie**nsan	p**ue**den	p**i**den

- Look at the six forms of the verb *pensar*. The stem of a regular verb would be *pens–*, but you can see that, for all forms of the verb except the 'we' and 'you plural' forms, the stem is *piens–*. This is the same for other common verbs of this type: *cerrar* (to close), *empezar* (to begin), *entender* (to understand), *querer* (to want), *preferir* (to prefer) and *perder* (to lose).
- When there are two 'e's in the stem, it is the second one that changes (*empiezo, prefiero, entiendo*).

  Pienso que es muy simpática.   I think she's very nice.
  Quieren ir al cine.   They want to go to the cinema.

- Now look at *poder*: the *o* of the stem changes to *ue* in all but the 'we' and 'you plural' forms of the verb. Other common verbs that follow this pattern are: *doler* (to hurt), *soler* (to usually do something), *dormir* (to sleep), *encontrar* (to find), *costar* (to cost), *volver* (to return), *acostarse* (to go to bed), *almorzar* (to have lunch).

  Me duele el estómago.   My stomach hurts.
  ¿Cuánto cuestan las botas?   How much do the boots cost?

- The verb *jugar* (to play) is also stem-changing, but in this case it is a *u* in the stem that changes to *ue* (*juego*, etc.).

  Juegan mucho al tenis.   They play tennis a lot.

- Verbs like *pedir* change the *e* of the stem to *i*, again in all but the 'we' and 'you plural' forms of the verb.

  Pido tapas en un restaurante español.   I order tapas in a Spanish restaurant.

The endings for stem-changing verbs are the same as for regular –*ar*, –*er*, and –*ir* verbs in the present tense.

1 **Choose the correct form of the verb to complete each sentence.**

⭐ Remember that in all tenses the 'we' form of the verb always ends –*mos* and the 'they' form always ends –*n*.

1 Mi amigo *prefiero / preferimos / prefiere* estar al aire libre.

2 Y tú, ¿siempre *cierra / cierras / cerráis* la puerta?

3 Yo no *puedo / podemos / puede* ir al cine hoy.

4 Nosotros *juegas / jugamos / jugáis* al bádminton después del insti.

5 A mí me *duelen / duelo / duele* la pierna.

6 Y vosotras, ¿cuándo *queréis / quieres / quieren* ver la tele?

7 Mi hermano y yo *sueles / solemos / suele* lavar el coche los sábados.

8 Las clases *empiezan / empiezas / empieza* a las nueve.

2 **Unjumble the stem-changing verbs in brackets to complete the sentences.**

1 Yo _____ (*reopiefr*) hacer equitación.

2 De vacaciones mi hermana _____ (*esule*) ir a Marbella.

3 Los españoles _____ (*anujge*) mucho al baloncesto.

4 Nosotros no _____ (*dpsmooe*) salir esta noche.

5 Y tú, ¿_____ (*useeqir*) poner la mesa?

3 Complete the following table with the missing forms of the stem-changing verbs.

	cerrar	jugar	preferir	volver
(yo)	cierro			vuelvo
(tú)		juegas	prefieres	
(él/ella/usted)	cierra		prefiere	
(nosotros/nosotras)		jugamos		volvemos
(vosotros/vosotras)	cerráis		preferís	volvéis
(ellos/ellas/ustedes)		juegan		

H 4 Complete these sentences with the correct form of one of the stem-changing verbs from page 40. The sentences must make sense.

1 Normalmente, cuando terminan las clases, yo .... a casa a las cuatro de la tarde.

2 Mi hermano .... salir con sus amigos, pero no .... porque .... muchos deberes.

3 Los billetes .... más de cien euros. ¡Nosotros no .... por qué!

4 Y tú, ¿cuántas horas .... por noche?

5 ¡Ay! Me .... la cabeza.

5 Translate these sentences into Spanish.

1 We play football at the weekend.

....

> Not all forms of stem-changing verbs have a spelling change. See p. 40.

2 She wants to go to the centre tomorrow.

....

> Remember, you can't say a el.

3 I prefer to watch films in the cinema.

....

H 6 Translate this passage into Spanish.

> Use the verb soler with the infinitive.

My friends usually go on holiday to France but my family and I prefer Spain. My brother always wants to do water sports and there are lots of different activities. The bad thing is that I usually drink too much cola and I often get stomach ache. I can't drink water because it's horrible.

> Remember that adjectives usually come after the noun they describe.

> Use lo with an adjective.

....

....

....

....

....

Verbs *Ser* and *estar*

» *Foundation p. 57*
» *Higher p. 60*

(G) The verbs *ser* and *estar* both mean 'to be'. They are both irregular verbs in the present tense.

They are used for different things.

	ser	estar
(yo)	soy	estoy
(tú)	eres	estás
(él/ella/usted)	es	está
(nosotros/nosotras)	somos	estamos
(vosotros/vosotras)	sois	estáis
(ellos/ellas/ustedes)	son	están

When to use *ser*

Ser is used for:

Description – when you want to describe a person or thing.

   *Yo **soy** alta pero mi hermano **es** muy bajo.*   **I am** tall but my brother **is** very short.

Origin – to say where someone comes from.

   ***Somos** de Ecuador.*   **We are** from Ecuador.

Characteristics to say what someone's character is like or what something is (always) like.

   *Mi insti **es** muy grande.*   My school **is** very big.

Time – to say what the time is.

   *Ahora **son** las seis de la mañana.*   **It is** now 6.00 a.m.

Occupation to say what job someone does.

   *Mis primos **son** profesores.*   My cousins **are** teachers.

Relationship – to talk about how people are related.

   *Y tú, ¿**eres** la tía de Juanita?*   **Are you** Juanita's aunt?

The word **DOCTOR** helps you to remember when to use *ser*.

When to use *estar*

Estar is used for:

Position – to say that someone is standing, sitting, etc.

   *¡Mira! **Están** sentados en el sofá.*   Look! **They are** sitting on the sofa.

Location – to say where something or someone is.

   *La estación **está** al lado del ayuntamiento.*   The station **is** next to the town hall.

Action – when you want to say what someone **is** doing.

   *¿Vosotros **estáis** copiando sus deberes?*   **Are you** copying her homework?

Condition – to say what state someone is in.

   *Después de tanto trabajo **estoy** muy cansado.*   After so much work **I am** very tired.

Emotion – to say how someone is feeling temporarily.

   *Pienso que **está** triste.*   I think **he is** sad.

The word **PLACE** helps you to remember when to use *estar*.

Sometimes, you can use *ser* and *estar* with the same adjective but the meaning is different. For example:

   ***ser** aburrido* – 'to be bor**ing**', <u>but</u> ***estar** aburrido* – 'to be bor**ed**'
   ***ser** listo* – 'to be clever', <u>but</u> ***estar** listo* – 'to be ready'

1 **Choose the correct form of *ser* or *estar*.**

   1 Yo *somos / eres / soy* alta.

   2 Juan y Miguel *son / somos / sois* hermanos.

   3 Nosotros *eres / sois / somos* de Barcelona.

   4 Y tú, ¿*está / estás / estamos* en el hotel?

   5 Las chicas *están / estamos / estáis* trabajando.

   6 Mi padre *estoy / estás / está* muy contento.

2 **Look at the sentences in exercise 1. For each one, say why *ser* or *estar* has been used. For the different uses, remember the letters from DOCTOR or PLACE from the grammar box.**

   Example: Mi madre es profesora. <u>Occupation</u>

   1 ....

   2 ....

   3 ....

   4 ....

   5 ....

   6 ....

3 Complete these sentences with the correct form of the verb *ser* or *estar*.
Remember to use the correct verb, according to the context.

1 Mi amigo Jaume _____ de Mallorca.

2 Yo _____ triste porque mi equipo ha perdido el partido.

3 ¿Dónde _____ tú?

4 Me gustan los chicos pero creo que _____ un poco egoístas.

5 Mi profesor dice que yo _____ perezoso, pero _____ trabajador en mi opinión.

6 En este momento nosotros _____ mirando ropa en Internet.

4 Translate these sentences into Spanish.

1 My favourite subject is history.

_____

2 Where are Manolo and José?   Is this position or origin?

_____

3 He's sitting next to his brother.   not *sentando*

_____

4 We are listening to the radio.

_____

5 They think we are from Scotland.

_____

H 5 Translate this passage into Spanish.   Are these characteristics or emotions?

My brother is quite tall and thin and he is always tired. It is because he works a lot at school and spends a
lot of time on his homework. However, he is very kind and sometimes he does my homework as well.
I'm a little selfish but I think it is great.

Be careful – you don't use *pequeño* in this context.

_____

_____

_____

_____

_____

Verbs The present tense: reflexive verbs

G Reflexive verbs often describe actions that you do to yourself (*lavarse* – to have a wash or wash yourself) or that you share with someone else (*pelearse* – to argue with each other). They are easily recognisable in their infinitive form because they have **–se** on the end (*divertirse*, etc.).

What makes these verbs different is that they need an extra word before the verb in any tense. This word is called the reflexive pronoun (*me, te, se, nos, os, se* depending on the form of the verb used – see p. 27 for a reminder).

	lavarse (to wash oneself)	**acostarse (to go to bed)**	**vestirse (to get dressed)**
(yo)	me lavo	me acuesto	me visto
(tú)	te lavas	te acuestas	te vistes
(él/ella/usted)	se lava	se acuesta	se viste
(nosotros/nosotras)	nos lavamos	nos acostamos	nos vestimos
(vosotros/vosotras)	os laváis	os acostáis	os vestís
(ellos/ellas/ustedes)	se lavan	se acuestan	se visten

Notice that *acostarse* (o → ue) and *vestirse* (e → i) are also stem-changing verbs. See pp. 40–41 for more information.

*¿A qué hora **te acuestas**?*	What time **do you go to bed**?
***Me acuesto** a las diez.*	**I go to bed** at 10.00.
***Se pelean** todo el tiempo.*	**They argue** all the time.
***Nos levantamos** temprano.*	**We get up** early.

When reflexive verbs are used in the infinitive, the reflexive pronoun is added on to the end of it. The pronoun must match the subject (the person who is doing the action):

| *Antes de vestir**me**, **tomo** el desayuno.* | Before **I** get dressed, **I** have breakfast. |

After a preposition (*a, de, en, con, sin*), you must use the infinitive of the verb. In the example above, the infinitive is **vestirme**. The reflexive pronoun on the end of the infinitive is **me**, because the subject of the verb is 'I'.

In this sentence, the reflexive pronoun on the infinitive is **se** because the subject is 'he':

| *Va al insti sin duchar**se**.* | **He**'s going to school without having a shower. |

1 Complete the sentences using the words from the box.

> te   lleva   levanto   nos   divertimos   se

1 Me _____ a las seis de la mañana.

2 Sus hermanas _____ pelean mucho.

3 Nos _____ cuando vamos al cine.

4 ¿Te bañas o _____ duchas?

5 Mi primo se _____ bien con todo el mundo.

6 De vacaciones mi familia y yo _____ quedamos en un hotel.

2 Match the sentence halves.

1 Mi mejor amigo y yo	**a** apoyamos si tenemos problemas.
2 Siempre nos	**b** quedarte en la playa?
3 Como tengo el pelo muy largo,	**c** levantarnos temprano mañana.
4 ¿Te gusta	**d** nos conocemos desde hace seis años.
5 Y vosotros,	**e** ¿os peleáis mucho?
6 Vamos a	**f** es bastante difícil peinarme.

3 Complete the sentences about Alfonso's day, using the pictures.

`7.00` `7.10` `7.30` `7.40` `22.00`

1 Alfonso se _____ a las siete.
2 A las siete y diez _____ _____.
3 _____ _____ a las siete y media.

4 Luego, a las ocho menos veinte, _____ _____.
5 Todas las noches _____ _____ a las diez.

4a Complete the sentences with the infinitive of the verb in brackets.

1 Después de _____ (levantarse) me ducho en el cuarto de baño.
2 Nos gusta _____ (divertirse) con los amigos.
3 ¿Vas a _____ (quedarse) en el mismo hotel este verano?
4 Son hermanos pero parece que les encanta _____ (pelearse).

> Don't forget to check the subject of the verb. Who's doing the action?

b Now translate the sentences into English.

1 _____
2 _____
3 _____
4 _____

5 Translate these sentences into Spanish.

> You need the 'we' form of the verb here.

1 My brother and I argue sometimes. _____
2 She normally gets up at seven o'clock. _____
3 They are going to stay in a hotel. _____

> With the infinitive of a reflexive verb, the pronoun is added to the end. See p. 44.

> Use antes de – remember, it is followed by the infinitive.

> Look back to direct object pronouns on p. 32.

H 6 Translate this passage into Spanish.

Every day, before going to bed, I read. It helps me to sleep better and then, when I get up in the morning, I am happy and I don't argue with my parents. However, my sister goes to bed late and gets on badly with our dad because she is always in a bad mood.

> The literal translation is 'of bad humour'.

G Verbs of opinion

In Spanish, many verbs for giving opinions need a pronoun like 'me'. In these structures, the person who likes / dislikes is actually the <u>indirect object</u> of the verb and the thing they like / dislike is the <u>subject</u>. To remember this, it might help you to think about what the Spanish literally means, for example:

Me gusta *el helado.*   I like ice cream.
(literally: The ice cream is pleasing to me.)

Les interesan *los idiomas.*   They are interested in languages.
(literally: Languages are interesting to them.)

The important things to remember:

•   Choose the correct pronoun to go before the verb (see the table below).

•   When these verbs are followed by a noun, check that the verb agrees with the noun.
They are simpler than other verbs – there are only **two** options:
  – 'he/she/it' form if what you like / dislike is singular (*me gusta*)
  – 'they' form if what you like / dislike is plural (*me gustan*)

me gusta / me gustan	I like	**nos gusta / nos gustan**	we like
te gusta / te gustan	you like (singular)	**os gusta / os gustan**	you like (plural)
le gusta / le gustan	he/she/it likes	**les gusta / les gustan**	they like
le gusta / le gustan	you like (singular, formal)	**les gusta / les gustan**	you like (plural, formal)

The following verbs of opinion behave in the same way as **gustar**:

encantar, chiflar, molar, flipar (to love/to be mad about), *interesar* (to be interested in), *apasionar* (to be passionate about), *molestar* (to bother), *fastidiar* (to annoy).

These verbs can also be followed by a verb. The second verb is in the infinitive form. The verb of opinion has the singular ending.

A (mi padre) *le chifla hacer deportes.*   My Dad loves doing sport.

> When you give the person who likes/dislikes (e.g. *mi padre*), the sentence needs to start with *A*.

To talk about things you liked / disliked in the past, use the preterite form of the verbs, e.g. *me **gustó**, me **gustaron**,* etc.

Le encantó la clase de ayer.   He loved the class yesterday.

Doler

Another verb which behaves like **gustar** is **doler**. You use this verb to say that something hurts.
Doler is a stem-changing verb in the present tense – *doler* → **duele** (see p. 40).

Me duele *la cabeza.*   My head hurts. (literally: The head hurts to me.)
¿Te duelen *las piernas?*   Do your legs hurt?

1 Circle the correct form to complete each sentence.

> ★ To work out which form of the verb you need, look carefully at the noun – singular or plural?

1   *Me gusta / Me gustan* tu chaqueta.

2   *Nos encanta / Nos encantan* las ciencias.

3   *Le chifla / Le chiflan* ir de compras.

4   *Me duele / Me duelen* los ojos.

5   *Les interesa / Les interesan* los cuadros.

2 Match these sentence halves.

1   A Pedro   **a**   nos gusta ver series en Netflix.

2   A ustedes   **b**   ¿Te gusta el baloncesto?

3   A mis amigos y yo   **c**   le gustan las películas de acción.

4   ¿Y a tí?   **d**   les gusta ir de vacaciones.

3 Complete these sentences with the correct verb form.

1 _____ el museo. (*interesar* – we)

2 Laura, ¿ _____ las canciones españolas? (*encantar* – you)

3 Jorge y Carolina, ¿ _____ hacer barbacoas? (*chiflar* – you plural)

4 _____ los deportes acuáticos. (*apasionar* – they)

5 No _____ quedarme en los albergues juveniles. (*gustar* – I)

6 No _____ la cabeza. (*doler* – she)

> ⭐ Remember the verb doesn't agree with the pronoun – the verb form is determined by whether the noun is singular or plural.

4a Choose four things and write your opinion of them, using the four verbs supplied.

el fútbol	los idiomas	llevar uniforme	las matemáticas
subir vídeos a Internet	la red	conocer a gente nueva	las historias de vampiros
los caramelos	los blogs	la tele	hacer deporte

1 (*flipar*) _____

2 (*molar*) _____

3 (*no gustar*) _____

4 (*no interesar*) _____

b Now translate your sentences into English.

1 _____

2 _____

3 _____

4 _____

5 Translate these sentences into Spanish.

> English doesn't use the definite article here, but you need it in Spanish.

1 I like fish but I don't like chips. _____

2 Do they love horror films? _____

3 Paula is not interested in going to the ice rink. _____

> What word do you need before 'Paula' in Spanish?

🄷 6 Translate this passage into Spanish.

I'm mad about books because they are a door to another world and I love using my imagination. My friend Paz really likes magazines but they don't interest me. The students at my school love the internet but I don't like it at all. When I surf the net, I have a headache after half an hour!

> Think about how you can use *doler* to say this.

_____

_____

_____

_____

Verbs The present tense: modal verbs

» Foundation p. 70, p. 92, p. 158
» Higher p. 76, p. 98, p. 161

(G) Poder, querer and soler

In Spanish there are a number of key verbs, known as **modal verbs**, that are very useful: *poder* (to be able to), *querer* (to want to) and *soler* (to usually/tend to) – learn these carefully and practise them frequently. (These are also stem-changing verbs – see pp. 40–41.)

	poder (to be able to)	querer (to want to)	soler (to usually/tend to)
(yo)	puedo	quiero	suelo
(tú)	puedes	quieres	sueles
(él/ella/usted)	puede	quiere	suele
(nosotros/nosotras)	podemos	queremos	solemos
(vosotros/vosotras)	podéis	queréis	soléis
(ellos/ellas/ustedes)	pueden	quieren	suelen

No **puedo** ir a la bolera.   I **can't** go to the bowling alley.
¿**Queréis** tomar algo?   Do you **want to** have something to eat or drink?
Solemos comer a las siete.   We **usually/tend to** eat at seven.

Se puede

You can use **se puede** to talk generally about what people 'can' do. If what you are talking about is a plural noun, you use the plural form of the verb, **se pueden**.

Se puede visitar la galería de arte.   You can visit the art gallery.
No se pueden alquilar bicis.   You can't hire bikes.

Se debe and se debería

To talk about what people 'must' or 'should' do, you use **se debe** (you/we must) and **se debería** (you/we should) followed by the infinitive. (*Se debería* is the conditional form – for more details, see pp. 64–65.)

Se debe comer fruta.   You/We **must** eat fruit.
Se debería ahorrar agua.   You/We **should** save water.

Tener que

Use **tener que** + infinitive to talk about what you 'have to' do. (For the present tense of *tener*, see p. 38.)

Tenemos que volver a casa.   **We have to** go home.

---

1 Circle the correct option to complete each sentence.

⭐ Think carefully about which form of the verb you need.

1 Ana no puede *usar / usa / uso* el ordenador de su hermano.

2 Suelen *ver / ve / vemos* la tele.

3 Quiero *salgo / salir / sale* el jueves.

4 Se pueden *visita / visitan / visitar* museos muy interesantes.

5 Se debería *apagáis / apaga / apagar* la luz.

2 Match these statements and responses. Then circle the infinitive in the verb + infinitive expressions in the second column.

⭐ What do all infinitive forms have in common?

⭐ In a matching activity, do all the ones you are sure about first. Then you will have fewer options to decide between for the more difficult ones.

1 ¡Estoy cansada!   a No se debe usar el móvil en el insti.

2 Tengo hambre.   b Suelo ir de compras.

3 Voy a mandar un SMS.   c Se debería reciclar el plástico.

4 Cuidamos el medio ambiente.   d ¿Quieres tomar una pizza?

5 ¿Que haces los sábados?   e Tienes que ir a la cama.

H 3 Find and correct the mistake in each sentence.

1 Quiero escucha música. ....

2 Se puede mandar correos. ....

3 ¿Sueles al cine? ....

4 No podemos venimos a la fiesta. ....

5 Tengo ir de compras. ....

6 Se deberían ducharse en vez de bañarse. ....

4 Complete these sentences with the correct form of the verb(s) in brackets, then translate the sentences into English.

1 ¿... al cine conmigo? (*do you want to go*)

....

2 .... los platos. (*I have to wash*)

....

3 .... piercings en el insti. (*you/we mustn't wear*)

....

4 Los hombres .... porque está lloviendo. (*can't go out*)

....

5 Translate these sentences into Spanish.

1 Can you go up the monument?

....

2 You should clean the kitchen.

....

3 I want to change room.

....

What form of the verb do you need after *can*?

Which verb do you need to say what people 'should' do in a general sense?

H 6 Translate this passage into Spanish.

Remember that in some Spanish expressions you don't need the article.

My friend Jorge spends too much time playing football with his friends. They usually go to the park after school. Today he will go back home late, so he won't be able to do his homework. Jorge wants to be a doctor and he should work harder. You have to study every day or you can't go to university.

Which tense do you need here?

What structure do you need when you are talking about what people 'must' do in a general sense?

....

....

....

....

....

(G) You use the preterite to talk about completed actions in the past.

Aprendí *a hacer vela.*   **I learned** how to sail.

¿Conociste *a algunas chicas en las vacaciones?*   **Did you meet** any girls during the holidays?

The preterite is <u>not</u> used for descriptions of things in the past or for repeated actions in the past – for these, you use the imperfect tense (see pp. 56–57).

There are two types of verbs: regular and irregular. **Regular verbs** have the same pattern of endings. **Irregular verbs** don't follow these patterns and have to be learned individually (see pp. 38–39).

To make the different preterite forms of regular verbs, remove *–ar*, *–er* or *–ir* from the infinitive of the verb to find the stem (the part that doesn't change). Then add the following endings to the stem:

	visit<u>ar</u> (to visit)	**com<u>er</u> (to drink)**	**sal<u>ir</u> (to leave/go out)**
(yo)	visit**é**	com**í**	sal**í**
(tú)	visit**aste**	com**iste**	sal**iste**
(él/ella/usted)	visit**ó**	com**ió**	sal**ió**
(nosotros/nosotras)	visit**amos**	com**imos**	sal**imos**
(vosotros/vosotras)	visit**asteis**	com**isteis**	sal**isteis**
(ellos/ellas/ustedes)	visit**aron**	com**ieron**	sal**ieron**

Recognising patterns

- In the preterite, endings for *–er* and *–ir* verbs are the same.
- The 'we' form of *–ar* and *–ir* verbs in the preterite is the same as the present tense: *visitamos* – we visit/we visited; *salimos* – we go out/we went out. You have to use the context to work out which is meant.

Exceptions

Some verbs are regular in the preterite apart from the 'I' form:

saqué (*sacar* – to take)   *toqué* (*tocar* – to touch/play [instrument])   *jugué* (*jugar* – to play [game/sport])

crucé (*cruzar* – to cross)   *empecé* (*empezar* – to begin)   *llegué* (*llegar* – to arrive)

Key time expressions

To help you recognise the preterite, look out for key time expressions such as *ayer* (yesterday) and *… pasado/a* (last …), e.g. *la semana pasada* (last week).

1 **Circle the verbs that are the same in the present tense and the preterite. Then highlight the other verbs that are in the preterite.**

⭐ Remember that some forms are the same in the present tense and the preterite.

hablaron	bebí	lavo	vivimos	compré	vende
cenamos	escribió	mando	viviste	bailasteis	tocamos
como	llamé	leí	necesitan	ordenáis	veo
cocinaste	aprendemos	lleva	salieron	recibió	

2 **Complete this grid with the correct verb forms.**

infinitive	present	preterite
	compro	
	partes	
	vende	
	tomamos	
	subís	
	beben	

3 Write the correct form of the verb in the preterite. Then translate into English.

1 permitir (*yo*) — permití — I ~~the permite~~ permitted

2 ganar (*él*) — ganó — She won

3 depender (*nosotros*) — dependimos — we depended.

4 comprender (*ustedes*) — comprendieron — they ~~understand~~ understood

5 recibir (*tú*) — recibiste — ~~y~~ you received

6 copiar (*ella*) — copió — She copied

4 Underline the verbs, then rewrite the sentences using the preterite.

1 Yo navego por Internet y él escribe una carta.

> Careful! What do you need to add to the stem to keep the hard 'g' sound?

2 No hablamos con ella porque sale temprano.

3 Mi hermano ayuda a mi madre pero ellos rompen los platos.

> What's the infinitive form of this verb? You need to know that to get the correct preterite ending.

5 Translate these sentences into Spanish.

1 In the café I ate a cake and drank a strawberry milkshake.

2 Ana and Jorge, did you visit your grandparents yesterday?

> Remember that you will need to add *a* after the verb here.

3 Last year my uncle and aunt sold their car and bought a motorbike.

H 6 Translate this passage into Spanish.

At Christmas we visited my grandparents. My grandmother cooked a delicious cake and my sisters prepared the food. We ate and drank a lot! Afterwards, my little sister danced and my cousins sang a very sad song. We received lots of presents from our family. I loved the present from my uncle – a very exciting book.

> Remember that encantar works like *gustar*.

(G) Some common verbs are irregular in the preterite and it is important that you know which they are and how they are formed. They don't follow a fixed pattern, so you need to learn them separately.

ser (to be)	ir (to go)	estar (to be)	hacer (to do, to make)	tener (to have)
fui	fui	estuve	hice	tuve
fuiste	fuiste	estuviste	hiciste	tuviste
fue	fue	estuvo	hizo	tuvo
fuimos	fuimos	estuvimos	hicimos	tuvimos
fuisteis	fuisteis	estuvisteis	hicisteis	tuvisteis
fueron	fueron	estuvieron	hicieron	tuvieron

poner (to put)	poder (to be able to)	venir (to come)	querer (to want)	decir (to say, to tell)
puse	pude	vine	quise	dije
pusiste	pudiste	viniste	quisiste	dijiste
puso	pudo	vino	quiso	dijo
pusimos	pudimos	vinimos	quisimos	dijimos
pusisteis	pudisteis	vinisteis	quisisteis	dijisteis
pusieron	pudieron	vinieron	quisieron	dijeron

The preterite of the verbs *ser* and *ir* is identical. This means that *fue*, for example, can mean either 'he/she/it was' or 'he/she/it went'. This is something to be aware of when you are translating from Spanish to English. In the context, it will always be clear which verb is being used. For instance, *fue* in the following sentence has to mean 'he went':

*El año pasado **fue** a Ibiza.*   Last year **he went** to Ibiza.

In this sentence, on the other hand, *fue* has to mean 'it was':

Fue *guay*   **It was** cool

The verb *poder* means 'to be able to'. In the preterite, therefore, it can translate as 'I was able to' etc. However, you would usually say 'I could'.

1 Match each Spanish verb to its English meaning.

1	I could	**a**	fui
2	we wanted	**b**	tuvisteis
3	they came	**c**	pude
4	she could	**d**	vinieron
5	he went	**e**	hicieron
6	I was	**f**	fue
7	they did	**g**	quisimos
8	you (informal plural) had	**h**	dijiste
9	you (singular) said	**i**	pudo

2 Correct the incorrect verbs in these sentences.
   Some of the sentences are correct.

   1 Mi amigo tuve que ir de vacaciones con sus padres. ....

   2 Hizo sol todos los días. ....

   3 Y tú, ¿fuisteis de vacaciones el verano pasado? ....

   4 Yo puso la mesa. ....

   5 Nosotros estuvimos en el restaurante anoche. ....

   6 La cena fui estupenda. ....

3 Complete these sentences with the correct verb in the preterite.

1 Mis amigos .... (*went*) a Gran Canaria.

2 Esta mañana .... (*it was*) calor.

Use the verb *hacer*.

3 El hombre .... (*wanted*) volver.

4 Nosotros .... (*came*) a tu casa.

5 Yo le .... (*told*) que María estaba enferma.

4 Rewrite these sentences in the correct order and then translate them into English.

1 y de vacaciones fui fotos saqué. ....

....

2 chico amigos a el quiso invitar sus. ....

....

3 mis que lo primos fue bueno vinieron. ....

....

4 pudo restaurante mi padrastro no al ir. ....

....

5 Translate these sentences into Spanish.

1 I went on holiday with my best friend last year.

Remember, you need the definite article here.

....

2 He did his homework at half past six.

In Spanish say 'the'.

....

3 They were in the same hotel.

....

6 Translate this passage into Spanish.

This is plural in Spanish.

Remember, *ser* and *ir* are identical in the preterite.

The best day of my holiday was Saturday, when my family and I went to Barcelona. The guide told us what to visit and we were able to see some interesting places. The best thing was the stadium and I took lots of photos there. When I returned home I put them up on my wall.

Object pronouns come before the verb.

....

....

....

....

Verbs The preterite: reflexive verbs

» Foundation p. 118
» Higher pp. 124–125

G Reflexive verbs behave in the same way as other verbs in the preterite, but they need a reflexive pronoun in front of the verb, just as they do in the present tense.

	–ar verbs lavarse (to get washed)	–er and –ir verbs aburrirse (to get bored)
(yo)	me lavé	me aburrí
(tú)	te lavaste	te aburriste
(él/ella/usted)	se lavó	se aburrió
(nosotros/nosotras)	nos lavamos	nos aburrimos
(vosotros/vosotras)	os lavasteis	os aburristeis
(ellos/ellas/ustedes)	se lavaron	se aburrieron

You use these verbs to say what someone did in the past in exactly the same situations that you use the preterite of non-reflexive verbs.

*Esta mañana **me levanté** a las ocho.*   This morning **I got up** at 8.00.
***Nos aburrimos** durante el concierto.*   **We got bored** during the concert.

1 Choose the correct form of the verb to complete each sentence.

1 Mi amigo *se lavó / me lavé / se lavaron* antes de salir.

2 Y tú, ¿cuándo *te despertaste / nos despertamos / me desperté*?

3 Yo *nos sentamos / se sentó / me senté* al lado de mi amigo.

4 Nosotros *se quejó / nos quejamos / os quejasteis* al director.

5 ¿Vosotros *se aburrieron / se aburrió / os aburristeis* en la clase?

6 Las chicas *se levantó / me levanté / se levantaron* tarde.

2 Write four sentences saying what you did yesterday and at what time, using the verbs in brackets.

1 (*despertarse*) ....

2 (*levantarse*) ....

3 (*sentarse*) ....

4 (*acostarse*) ....

3 Translate these sentences into Spanish.

1 We got bored during the match.

....

> Use the verb *aburrirse*. This will be translated by just two Spanish words.

2 They woke up early.

....

3 Did you have a shower this morning?

....

> Use the verb *ducharse*. This will also be translated by two words in Spanish.

Verbs The preterite: stem-changing verbs

G Some –ir verbs are stem-changing in the preterite. They have a vowel change, as you can see in the following table. The changes only occur in the 'he/she' and 'they' forms of these verbs.

preferir	dormir	morir	pedir	seguir	reírse	vestirse
preferí	dormí	morí	pedí	seguí	me reí	me vestí
preferiste	dormiste	moriste	pediste	seguiste	te reíste	te vestiste
prefirió	durmió	murió	pidió	siguió	se rió	se vistió
preferimos	dormimos	morimos	pedimos	seguimos	nos reímos	nos vestimos
preferisteis	dormisteis	moristeis	pedisteis	seguisteis	os reísteis	os vestisteis
prefirieron	durmieron	murieron	pidieron	siguieron	se rieron	se vistieron

Durmió en el tren. He slept on the train.   *Prefirieron ir al cine.* They preferred to go to the cinema.

1 Rewrite these sentences in the correct order.

1 durmieron viaje las durante chicas el.

....

2 años murió mi abuelo tres hace.

....

3 el reí me amigo patio cuando cayó en mi.

....

4 se cuarto en baño el vistió de.

....

5 calamares restaurante pidió en Manuel el.

....

6 a porque prefirieron la cerca ir bolera está.

....

2 Write a sentence using the preterite of each of the verbs in brackets.

1 (*seguir*) ....

2 (*vestirse*) ....

3 (*pedir*) ....

4 (*preferir*) ....

3 Translate these sentences into Spanish.

Use the verb *pedir*.

1 I ordered the chicken. ....

2 My cat died last year. ....

3 They laughed during the film. ....

Be careful – not every verb in the preterite is stem-changing in this passage.

Use the preterite of *vestirse*.

H 4 Translate this passage into Spanish.

Last weekend my best friend, Isabel, went to Blackpool with her family. She got up early and got dressed immediately. They went by car to the coast and followed the directions on the map. She preferred the visit to the theme park. On the way home, Isabel slept for two hours in the car.

'On the way to' is *De camino a*.

Translate this as 'during'.

....

....

....

(G) The imperfect tense is a past tense and is used for the following:

* to <u>describe</u> something or someone in the past

  *El hombre **era** muy alto.*   The man **was** very tall.

* to say what someone <u>was doing</u> or what was happening

  ***Hacía** mis deberes cuando mi amigo llamó.*   **I was doing** my homework when my friend called.

* to say what someone <u>used to do</u> or what things used to be like.

  *De niño, **jugaba** con mi perro.*   As I child, **I used to play** with my dog.

There are two sets of endings, one for –*ar* verbs and one for –*er* and –*ir* verbs. Take off the last two letters of the infinitive and add the following endings:

	–ar verbs hablar	–er verbs comer	–ir verbs vivir
(yo)	habl**aba**	com**ía**	viv**ía**
(tú)	habl**abas**	com**ías**	viv**ías**
(él/ella/usted)	habl**aba**	com**ía**	viv**ía**
(nosotros/nosotras)	habl**ábamos**	com**íamos**	viv**íamos**
(vosotros/vosotras)	habl**abais**	com**íais**	viv**íais**
(ellos/ellas/ustedes)	habl**aban**	com**ían**	viv**ían**

There are only three verbs that are irregular in the imperfect tense:

ser (to be)		ir (to go)		ver (to see)	
era	éramos	iba	íbamos	veía	veíamos
eras	erais	ibas	ibais	veías	veíais
era	eran	iba	iban	veía	veían

1 Choose the correct form of the verb(s) to complete each sentence.

1 Elena *vivíamos / vivía / vivías* en Perú cuando *eras / eran / era* joven.

2 Mi hermano y yo *estabais / estábamos / estaban* en el parque.

3 Yo siempre *jugaba / jugábamos / jugaban* al fútbol con mis amigos.

4 Cuando Raúl *estabas / estaban / estaba* de vacaciones, *hacías / hacía / hacían* submarinismo cada día.

2 Complete these sentences with a verb from the box that makes sense. You don't need all the words. Then translate the sentences into English.

1 El hotel _____ una piscina enorme.

_____

2 En su tiempo libre, Julia _____ artes marciales.

_____

3 Nosotros _____ tiro con arco cada día.

_____

4 Mi madre _____ a caballo cuando era niña.

_____

5 ¿ _____ de pesca mucho?

_____

6 En el camping donde me alojaba, no _____ muchas personas.

ibas	practicaba
éramos	marcábamos
había	tenía
jugaba	montaba
hacíamos	estabas

¡Viva! GCSE Spanish © Pearson Education Limited 2017

H 3 **Rewrite this text about Leonardo's free time using the imperfect tense to say what he used to do. The first sentence has been started for you.**

Leonardo hace muchas cosas en su tiempo libre. Los sábados siempre sale con sus amigos y normalmente van al cine. Practica muchos deportes también y su favorito es el baloncesto. Escucha música en la radio cuando está en casa y usa el ordenador. A veces le gusta descansar y lee un libro antes de dormirse.

Cuando era más joven, Leonardo

....

....

....

....

H 4 **Write five sentences to say what you used to do in your free time. Use five of these verbs in the imperfect tense: *jugar, ir, ver, practicar, hacer, descansar, leer, escuchar, salir.***

1 ....

2 ....

3 ....

4 ....

5 ....

5 **Translate these sentences into Spanish.**

1 She was reading a magazine in the lounge.

....

2 The woman was quite tall and she had blue eyes.

....

> Use the imperfect tense of *ser* – describing someone in the past.

3 There wasn't a lot of space on the campsite.

....

> Remember that the *no* comes before the verb.

H 6 **Translate this passage into Spanish.**

> Use the preterite for a completed action in the past.

> Use the imperfect tense to say what someone was doing.

Last year I went on holiday to Marbella. The hotel where I was staying had a fantastic restaurant and the waiters were very nice. There were also some pretty gardens where I used to read a magazine every morning. My parents say that next year we are going to go back to the hotel.

> Use the immediate future tense (part of the verb *ir* + *a* + the infinitive). 'To go back' – 'to return'.

....

....

....

....

....

Verbs Preterite or imperfect tense?

» *Foundation pp. 136–137*
» *Higher pp. 142–143*

Ⓖ The preterite and the imperfect tense have different meanings and uses in Spanish:

- You use the preterite to talk about <u>completed actions</u> in the past (see pp. 50–55).
- You use the imperfect tense to describe what things <u>were like</u> or what someone <u>was doing</u>, what someone <u>did repeatedly</u>, what someone <u>used to do</u> or what something <u>used to be like</u> (see pp. 56–57).

The challenge is to know which to use and how to use them together. Combining the preterite with the imperfect in your speaking and writing will allow you to produce work that is more complex and descriptive.

For example, you might want to say what **was happening** (imperfect) when another action <u>took place</u> (preterite).

__Hablaba__ por Skype cuando <u>recibí</u> un mensaje de mi amigo.
I was talking on Skype when <u>I received</u> a message from my friend.

You could turn the sentence around, but the verbs would remain the same:

Cuando <u>recibí</u> un mensaje de mi amigo, __hablaba__ por Skype.
When <u>I received</u> a message from my friend, **I was talking** on Skype.

When writing descriptions in the past, you will often need to use both tenses:

__Estaba__ muy contento porque mi equipo de rugby <u>ganó</u> el final.
I was really happy because my rugby team <u>won</u> the final.

When considering which tense to use, it can be helpful to picture the trace of a heartbeat; the constant horizontal line being the imperfect tense and the interrupting beat being a completed action in the preterite.

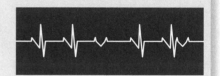

1 Write which tense you would use to translate these sentences.

Example: She was tall. imperfect

1 I saw the match. ....
2 He was crying. ....
3 They used to work. ....

4 We fell over. ....
5 Every day I helped my boss. ....
6 I arrived late. ....

2 Circle the verb in the correct tense to complete these sentences.

★ Look out for time markers to help you identify completed actions in the past.

1 El primer día *conocí / conocía* a mi jefe y no *fue / era* nada simpático.
2 El fin de semana pasado *nos alojamos / nos alojábamos* en un hotel que *estuvo / estaba* en la costa.
3 *Hablé / Hablaba* con mi hermano por teléfono cuando mi padre *llegó / llegaba* a casa.
4 *Montaba / Monté* en bici cuando *vi / veía* a mi amigo.
5 Cuando *tuve / tenía* diez años, *fui / iba* a un concierto de Adele.

3 Put the verb in brackets into the correct form of either the imperfect or the preterite tense.

1 El hotel .... (*tener*) una piscina. Sin embargo no .... (*nadar*) porque no me gusta hacer natación.
2 El año pasado mis amigos y yo .... (*ir*) a Italia y la gente .... (*ser*) muy amable.
Ⓗ 3 Yo .... (*pasear*) al perro en el parque cuando .... (*conocer*) a un chico guapo.
Ⓗ 4 Mis padres .... (*ver*) la tele cuando yo .... (*llamar*).

★ Each sentence has one verb in the preterite and one verb in the imperfect.

4 Translate the sentences you have completed in exercise 3 into English.

1 ....

2 ....

(H) 3 ....

(H) 4 ....

> ⭐ Remember that *hacer* can mean 'to go' when used with sports.

> ⭐ There are lots of ways to translate the imperfect tense. Use the context to work out what it needs to be in English.

5 Translate the following sentences into Spanish using the correct tense (imperfect or preterite).

1 They played tennis every day. ....

2 I used to wake up early. ....

3 They played tennis last weekend. ....

4 I didn't wake up late yesterday. ....

> Remember to include the correct reflexive pronoun.

> Put *no* before the reflexive pronoun to make this negative.

> ⭐ In question 1, look out for a phrase that cannot be translated word for word!

(H) 6 Now translate these sentences into Spanish.

1 I was hungry so I ate a sandwich.

....

> Use *así que* here.

2 It was raining when he went out with his friends.

....

3 Six years ago, when I was in Paris, I lost my passport.

....

> Use *Hace* + time here.

> ⭐ To help you decide which tense to use, keep in mind the heartbeat line; is the verb describing something, saying what used to happen or is it a single event in the past?

(H) 7 Translate this passage into Spanish

> You need *de* here.

> You need *mientras* here.

When I lived in Madrid I went on holiday to the coast. One day, while I was sunbathing on the beach, I saw Rafa Nadal. He had brown eyes, long hair and was very tall. Unfortunately, I used to be quite shy and I didn't say anything!

> Remember to include the personal *a*.

> This verb is irregular in the preterite.

> Remember to include the definite article with body parts.

....

....

....

....

Verbs The near future tense

» *Foundation pp. 34–35*
» *Higher pp. 38–39, p. 82*

(G) You use the near future tense to talk about what you are <u>going to do</u> in the future. To form it, use the present tense of *ir* + *a* + infinitive.

pronoun	present tense of *ir*	*a*	infinitive
(yo)	voy		leer
(tú)	vas		visitar
(él/ella/usted)	va	a	comer
(nosotros/nosotras)	vamos		salir
(vosotros/vosotras)	vais		nadar
(ellos/ellas/ustedes)	van		usar

¿Qué **vamos a hacer?**   What **are we going to do?**
Voy a ir al cine.   I'm **going to go** to the cinema.

Key time expressions

To help you recognise the near future tense, look out for key time expressions like these:

mañana	tomorrow	*este fin de semana*	this weekend
... que viene	next...	e.g. *el año que viene*	next year
... próximo/a	next...	e.g. *la semana próxima*	next week

1 **Circle the correct form to complete the verbs in the near future tense. Then highlight the infinitives.**

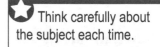 Think carefully about the subject each time.

1 Jorge, ¿*vas / voy* a salir con tus amigos?

2 Isabel *va / vais* a ir de paseo.

3 Mis amigos y yo *vas / vamos* a hacer los deberes.

4 Yo *voy / van* a chatear.

5 Ana y Mateo, ¿*vais / va* a ver la televisión?

6 Los miembros del equipo *van / vamos* a llegar a las dos.

2 **Complete the text using the words from the box.**

Why does this have a capital letter? Use all the clues you can find to help you work out the answers!

van	ir	salir	voy	a	Vamos	va

El sábado que viene voy a **1** _____ con Ana. **2** _____ a quedar

en su casa y después vamos **3** _____ ir de compras. Después vamos a

4 _____ a la cafetería con nuestras amigas Alba y Cristina. Yo

5 _____ a tomar un helado de chocolate pero Ana no

6 _____ a comer un helado. Prefiere las tartas de queso. Alba y Cristina

7 _____ a beber una cola.

3 **Underline the verbs in the present tense and rewrite the sentences using the near future tense.**

Hoy ... **1** voy a la playa. El verano que viene ... .

      2 mi hermana ve un partido. ....

      3 mis padres sacan fotos. ....

      4 acampamos en el jardín. ....

      5 no lees esta revista. ....

      6 ¿visitáis el museo? ....

⭐ Look carefully at the English pronouns to work out the correct form of the verb in Spanish.

4 **Complete the Spanish sentences using the correct form of the near future tense. Then complete the English translations.**

1 ¡................ ser estupendo! **3** Ana, ¿qué .... beber?

It's .... great! Ana, what are you .... ?

2 ¿A qué hora .... llegar? **4** .... hacer una visita guiada.

When are they .... ? We're .... a guided tour.

⭐ Look carefully at the verb form to work out the subject – remember, if there are two verbs in a sentence, the subject may not be the same for each verb.

5 **Translate these sentences into Spanish.**

1 I'm not going to go out with my friends because I'm tired.

....

2 They're going to chat online tonight.

....

3 We're going to do sightseeing but my parents are going to relax.

....

H 6 **Translate this passage into Spanish.**

Translate this as 'students of German'.

Next year, my girlfriend, Ana, is going to travel for six months but I'm going to go to university where I'm going to study languages. All the people studying German are going to live in Germany for nearly a year. We're going to get to know lots of young people and I'm going to improve my German.

Thinking of synonyms in English can help you if you can't remember the Spanish word right away – e.g. 'improve' means 'get better'.

....

....

....

....

G You use the future tense to say what someone <u>will do</u> or what <u>will happen</u>. It is formed by adding the following endings to the infinitive of the verb (the form that ends *–ar*, *–er* or *–ir*). The good news is that the same endings are used for all verbs. Here they are with the verb *comprar* (to buy):

(yo) comprar**é**	(nosotros/as) comprar**emos**
(tú) comprar**ás**	(vosotros/as) comprar**éis**
(él/ella/usted) comprar**á**	(ellos/ellas/ustedes) comprar**án**

Irregular verbs

There are some irregular verbs whose future tense stem is not the infinitive. Here are the most common ones with their stem. Remember that the stem is what you add the endings to.

verb	meaning	future tense stem
poner	to put	pondr–
decir	to say, to tell	dir–
saber	to know	sabr–
venir	to come	vendr–
querer	to want	querr–
salir	to leave, to go out	saldr–
hacer	to do, to make	har–
tener	to have	tendr–
poder	to be able to	podr–

⭐ The future of **hay** (there is/are) is **habrá** (there will be).

*Este año **iré** de vacaciones a España.* This year **I will go** on holiday to Spain.
*Creo que **lloverá**.* I think **it will rain**.
*Mis amigos **vendrán** conmigo.* My friends **will come** with me.

---

1 **Tick the <u>four</u> sentences that contain verbs in the future tense.**

1 Este fin de semana mi amiga visitará a sus abuelos. ☐

2 En el futuro nosotros sacaremos más fotos. ☐

3 Llueve mucho aquí. ☐

4 Compré un nuevo móvil esta mañana. ☐

5 ¿Pasarás toda la mañana en la playa? ☐

6 Siempre veo a mis tíos en la cafetería. ☐

7 ¿Tendréis la oportunidad de asistir a un colegio español? ☐

8 Hice deporte ayer. ☐

2a **Unjumble the words in brackets to complete the sentences.**

1 Enrique _____ (*rgeálal*) a las ocho.

2 Creo que _____ (*raháb*) muchas personas en la playa.

3 Mis padres _____ (*nnárdaa*) todo el día en la piscina del hotel.

4 ¿Tú _____ (*rsaeáhcucs*) música rock en el concierto?

5 Yo nunca _____ (*réi*) de vacaciones a Estados Unidos.

6 Nuria y yo _____ (*osn lamsoarejo*) en un hotel.

This is a reflexive verb.

b Now translate the sentences from exercise 2a into English.

1 ....

2 ....

3 ....

4 ....

5 ....

6 ....

H 3 Change the verb in brackets from the present tense to the future tense.

1 Durante la visita a la Alhambra, vosotros .... (*visitáis*) unos jardines bonitos.

2 Estoy cansada. Creo que .... (*me acuesto*) pronto.

3 Juan odia los mosquitos y .... (*usa*) repelente de mosquitos el próximo año.

4 El centro comercial es muy popular, así que .... (*hay*) mucha gente allí.

H 4 Write a sentence using any verb in the future tense as well as the word(s) in brackets. Use a different verb in each sentence.

1 (*vacaciones*) ....

2 (*genial*) ....

3 (*viento*) ....

4 (*un mensaje*) ....

H 5 Translate these sentences into Spanish.

1 We will arrive at half past ten.

....

2 They will be able to sunbathe next to the pool.

....

> Check the irregular verb table.

3 It will be sunny every day.

> You don't use the verb *ser* or *estar* here.

....

H 6 Translate this passage into Spanish.

> This is just one word in Spanish.

According to the forecast, it will rain a lot tomorrow, so we will not go to the beach. My parents say we will go to the museum, which is in the centre. It will be very boring. Later I will go to the shops with my cousin and we will buy presents for our friends.

> *por* or *para*?

> *ser aburrido* – 'to be boring'
> *estar aburrido* – 'to be bored'

....

....

....

....

....

G The conditional is used to say what someone <u>would do</u> or what <u>would happen</u> in the future. Endings are added on to the infinitive of the verb and irregular stems are exactly the same as they are for the future tense (see p. 62).

	comprar (to buy)
(yo)	comprar**ía**
(tú)	comprar**ías**
(él/ella/usted)	comprar**ía**
(nosotros/nosotras)	comprar**íamos**
(vosotros/vosotras)	comprar**íais**
(ellos/ellas/ustedes)	comprar**ían**

*Su casa es bastante bonita pero yo **cambiaría** los muebles.*
His house is quite nice but **I would change** the furniture.

***Pondrían** la televisión en el salón pequeño.*
They would put the TV in the small lounge.

*No **iríamos** al Caribe sin mucho dinero.*
We wouldn't go to the Caribbean without lots of money.

The conditional form of *haber* is **habría** – 'there would be'.

The conditional can be used to express desires for the future by using the verb *gustar* followed by an infinitive:

    ***Me gustaría** enseñar inglés.*   **I would like** to teach English.

H A useful construction is *se debería* plus the infinitive of a verb, which means 'you/we should' or 'you/we ought to' do something.

    ***Se debería** ahorrar energía.*   **You/we should** save energy.
    ***No se debería** usar bolsas de plástico.*   **You/we shouldn't** use plastic bags.

---

1 **Match the sentence halves. Then translate the underlined verbs into English.**

1 <u>Me gustaría</u>   **a** el sistema de transporte público.   ....

2 En mi ciudad, <u>yo mejoraría</u>   **b** en el campo.   ....

3 Mis amigos   **c** ser azafata.   ....

4 <u>Preferiría</u> ir   **d** <u>cambiarían</u> los muebles viejos.   ....

5 <u>No podríamos</u> vivir   **e** a Mallorca.   ....

H 2 **Write the correct form of the conditional of the verb in brackets.**

1 Yo .... (*ir*) a la universidad.

2 Nosotros .... (*ayudar*) a nuestra tía.

3 ¿Tú .... (*aprender*) un nuevo idioma?

4 Mis padres .... (*cambiar*) el color de la cocina.

5 ¿Vosotros .... (*trabajar*) en España?

6 Lucas no .... (*hacer*) nada.

H 3 There are five conditional form mistakes in this passage. Find and circle them, then rewrite the passage with your corrections.

> Me gustarían trabajar en el extranjero porque serían una oportunidad fantástica de ver otras culturas. También ganarían dinero y podrían visitar el resto del país los fines de semana. Viajarías en coche a muchos sitios diferentes.

....

....

....

....

H 4 Write four sentences saying what should be done to improve where you live. Begin each one with *Se debería*.

1 ....

2 ....

3 ....

4 ....

H 5 Translate these sentences into Spanish.

1 I would like to go to France.

....

> Which form of the verb do you use here?

2 We would buy a flat in the centre.

....

3 I think they would live in the countryside.

....

> Remember that in Spanish you have to say 'I think that'.

H 6 Translate this passage into Spanish.

> Remember that adjectives usually come after the noun.

I would like to take a gap year in Central America. It would be a fantastic experience! I would teach English to young children and I would learn a lot about their culture. I would work many hours but it would be great. I would go back to my country after nine months.

> This is the same as 'to return'.

> Translate this as 'of'.

....

....

....

....

(G) The present continuous tense is used to say what someone <u>is doing</u> or what <u>is happening</u>. It is formed by using the present tense of the verb *estar* (to be) + the present participle.

This is the present tense of the verb *estar*:

	estar (to be)
(yo)	estoy
(tú)	estás
(él/ella/usted)	está
(nosotros/nosotras)	estamos
(vosotros/vosotras)	estáis
(ellos/ellas/ustedes)	están

The present participle is formed as follows:

–ar verbs: remove the *–ar* from the infinitive and add **–ando**
  hablar → *habl* → **hablando**

–er and –ir verbs: remove the *–er* or *–ir* from the infinitive and add **–iendo**

  beber → *beb* → **bebiendo**   *vivir* → *viv* → **viviendo**

  Estamos hablando español.   **We are speaking** Spanish.
  ¿Qué **estás haciendo**?   What **are you doing**?

Notice that the *–ando* and *–iendo* have the meaning of '–ing' in English.

Here are some of the most common irregular present participles:

  decir → diciendo   *dormir* → durmiendo   *leer* → leyendo   *pedir* → pidiendo

In English, we often use a present participle where in Spanish an infinitive is used:

  *Me gusta **jugar** al tenis.*   I like **playing** tennis.
  *Les interesa **visitar** museos.*   They are interested in **visiting** museums.

This is something you should look out for when translating from English into Spanish.

1a Say whether these sentences contain a verb in the present continuous (PC) or simple present tense (P)?

1 Estoy viendo la televisión. _____

2 Siempre repaso para mis exámenes. _____

3 ¿Estás escuchando la radio? _____

4 Trabajan todo el día. _____

5 Está escribiendo un correo electrónico. _____

6 Estoy preparando la cena. _____

b Now translate the sentences into English.

1 _____

2 _____

3 _____

4 _____

5 _____

6 _____

2 Write the present participle for these verbs.

1 preparar _____   4 leer _____   7 ayudar _____

2 hacer _____   5 ver _____   8 decir _____

3 aprender _____   6 dormir _____   9 escribir _____

3 **Write the correct form of the present continuous of the verb in brackets.**

1 Yo _____ (*preparar*) la cena.

2 Antonio _____ (*esperar*) a sus amigos.

3 Mis primos _____ (*ayudar*) a sus padres.

4 ¿Tú _____ (*hacer*) el vago?

5 Mi hermano y yo _____ (*escribir*) una carta.

4 **Make sentences using the present continuous tense and the person of the verb given.**

Example: tú / hacer ¿Qué estás haciendo aquí?

1 yo / jugar _____

2 nosotros / ver _____

3 vosotros / leer _____

4 ellos / repasar _____

5 él / tomar _____

5 **Translate these sentences into Spanish.**

Esperar means 'to wait <u>for</u>', so you don't need *por* or *para*.

1 I am waiting for the bus. _____

2 We are eating a sandwich. _____

3 Bea and Tom are jogging. _____

4 She is sleeping in her room. _____

Remember that this is irregular.

H 6 **Translate this passage into Spanish.**

You don't need to translate 'about' here, it's part of the verb.

'Starting' is not in the present continuous. What part of the verb should you use?

I am thinking about starting a new sport because I want to go out more. At the moment I am lazing around too much and I don't like it. It's Saturday and my friends are doing sports. Ana is playing tennis, Lucía is swimming and Elena is jogging. I'm watching TV!

You don't need to translate 'it' here.

Use *hacer el vago* here.

_____

_____

_____

_____

_____

_____

G
H The imperfect continuous tense is used to say what someone <u>was doing</u> or what <u>was happening</u>. It is formed by using the imperfect tense of the verb *estar* (to be) + the present participle.

	imperfect tense of estar (to be)	the present participle
(yo)	estaba	**–ar verbs**
(tú)	estabas	remove the *–ar* from the
(él/ella/usted)	estaba	infinitive and add *–ando:*
(nosotros/nosotras)	estábamos	*hablar* ➔ *habl* ➔ ***hablando***
(vosotros/vosotras)	estabais	**–er and –ir verbs**
(ellos/ellas/ustedes)	estaban	remove the *–er or –ir* from the
		infinitive and add *–iendo:*
		beber ➔ *beb* ➔ ***bebiendo***

See p. 66 for more on how to form the present participle.

Estaban viendo *la tele.*   **They were watching** TV.
Estaba nevando *en las montañas.*   **It was snowing** in the mountains.
Estábamos escuchando *la radio.*   **We were listening** to the radio.

The imperfect and the imperfect continuous tenses are translated the same way into English:

Estaban viendo/Veían la tele.   They were watching TV.

H 1 Choose the correct word to complete each sentence.

1 Mis amigos y yo *estaba / estábamos / estaban* jugando al fútbol.

2 ¿Tú *estabais / estaban / estabas* escuchando?

3 Yo *estaba / estaban / estabas* bebiendo limonada.

4 Carla *estaba / estabas / estábamos* trabajando.

H 2 Match the sentence halves.

1 De vacaciones, nosotros	a estaba tomando paella.
2 Cuando entré en el salón,	b estábamos tomando el sol todo el día.
3 Los alumnos estaban	c entre Londres y Barcelona.
4 El avión estaba volando	d estudiando en el recreo.
5 En el restaurante,	e mi padre estaba leyendo el periódico.

H 3 Rewrite these jumbled sentences in the correct order.

1 estaban al mis baloncesto hermanas jugando _____

2 conduciendo coche mi el padre estaba _____

3 Madrid en estaba no nevando _____

4 un mi cenando estaba restaurante con en novia _____

5 ensayando concierto clásica estábamos de para un música

H 4a Finish the sentences with your own answers. The first word each time should be a present participle.

1 De vacaciones, Juanita estaba

2 Cuando la vi, estaba

3 María y yo estábamos

4 Los chicos estaban

5 ¿Estabas

H b Now translate the sentences from 4a into English.

1

2

3

4

5

H 5 Translate these sentences into Spanish.

1 They were helping in the kitchen.

2 Ana was driving her new car.

> This adjective comes before the noun when it means 'brand new'.

3 What were you doing?

> Think of this as 'you were doing'.

H 6 Translate this passage into Spanish.

> You don't need an extra word here – the verb you need means 'to look for'.

> Use the imperfect tense here.

Isabel was looking on the internet for an article about the environment because she had to do some homework for geography. She was thinking of writing about homeless people in Africa. She asked her older brother, who was working in his room. He showed her an interesting article.

> Remember, you always use the infinitive after a preposition.

> Think about the position of the object pronoun.

(G) The perfect tense is used to say what someone <u>has done</u> or what <u>has happened</u>. It is formed by using the present tense of the verb *haber* (to have) + the past participle.

This is the present tense of *haber*:

	haber (to have)
(yo)	he
(tú)	has
(él/ella/usted)	ha
(nosotros/nosotras)	hemos
(vosotros/vosotras)	habéis
(ellos/ellas/ustedes)	han

The past participle is formed as follows:

–ar verbs: remove the *–ar* from the infinitive and add **–ado**

mirar ➜ mir ➜ **mirado**

Esta mañana **he trabajado** *duro.*   This morning **I have worked** hard.

–er and –ir verbs: remove the *–er* or *–ir* from the infinitive and add **–ido**

comer ➜ com ➜ **comido**   vivir ➜ viv ➜ **vivido**
¿Has aprendido mucho?   **Have you learned** a lot?
Hemos escrito una carta.   **We have written** a letter.

Here are the most common irregular past participles:

infinitive	past participle		infinitive	past participle
escribir	escrito		romper	roto
ver	visto		abrir	abierto
hacer	hecho		volver	vuelto
poner	puesto		morir	muerto
decir	dicho			

Other past participles have an accent on the *i*:

leer ➜ leído   oír ➜ oído   traer ➜ traído

1 Tick the three sentences that contain an irregular past participle.

1 He decidido subir unos vídeos. ☐   4 Han llegado tarde. ☐

2 No he visto el programa. ☐   5 Mi pez ha muerto. ☐

3 He roto mi móvil. ☐

2 Choose the correct form of *haber* to complete these sentences.

1 ¿Tú *has / habéis / han* hecho todo?   4 Nosotros *habéis / han / hemos* visto el vídeo.

2 Yo *hemos / he / has* leído esa novela.   5 ¿Vosotros *habéis / han / hemos* estado enfermos?

3 Pepe y Fátima *has / han / he* ido al cine.   6 Mi amiga *hemos / ha / has* comido en un restaurante chino.

3a Write out these sentences, changing the verb in brackets to the past participle.

1 He (*jugar*) a un videojuego.

....

2 Carolina ha (*compartir*) fotos en Facebook.

....

3 Han (*ver*) la última película de Leonardo DiCaprio.

....

4 ¿Has (*comprar*) un regalo para tu madre?

....

b **Now translate the sentences from exercise 3a into English.**

1 ....

2 ....

3 ....

4 ....

4 **Answer these questions in full sentences, using the perfect tense.**

1 ¿Cuántas aplicaciones has descargado esta semana?

....

2 ¿Adónde has ido recientemente con tus amigos?

....

3 ¿Qué música has escuchado esta semana?

....

4 ¿Qué ha hecho tu mejor amigo/a hoy?

....

5 **Translate these sentences into Spanish.**

> This has to agree
> with a feminine noun.

1 I have seen an amazing film.

....

2 They have returned early.

....

3 We haven't used Twitter.

....

> Remember: to make a verb negative, put *no* before the form of *haber*.

H **6** **Translate this passage into Spanish.**

> Use the present participle.

Recently I have spent a lot of time sending messages to friends and family. For example, this morning I have sent emails to my friends in Spain. I've also written a letter to my grandmother. She doesn't have access to the internet and, besides, she would prefer to read a letter because it's more personal.

> Use the conditional tense.

> Remember, this is irregular.

....

....

....

....

....

....

The pluperfect tense is used to say what someone <u>had done</u> or what <u>had happened</u> at a particular moment in the past.

Using the pluperfect tense means that you can talk about events in the past in more detail. Using this tense correctly will add variety and complexity to your speaking and writing.

The pluperfect tense is formed by using the imperfect tense of the verb *haber* (to have) + the past participle. Here is the imperfect tense of *haber*:

	haber (to have)
(yo)	había
(tú)	habías
(él/ella/usted)	había
(nosotros/nosotras)	habíamos
(vosotros/vosotras)	habíais
(ellos/ellas/ustedes)	habían

See p. 70 for how to form the past participle and for a list of common irregulars.

*Creía que **había perdido** mi bolso.*   I thought that **I had lost** my handbag.
***Habían salido** diez minutos antes.*   **They had left** ten minutes before.
***Habíamos pensado** que sería fácil.*   **We had thought** it would be easy.

1 Highlight the past participle in these sentences.

1 La última vez que la vi, había dejado de jugar al tenis.

2 Manolo había decidido salir temprano.

3 ¿Qué habías comprado para su cumpleaños?

4 Me había dicho que iba a la fiesta.

5 No habíamos escrito nada en los cuadernos.

6 Había comido antes de la una.

2 Translate these sentences into English.

1 Yo había jugado mal. _____

2 Habíamos trabajado mucho. _____

3 Habían sido felices. _____

4 Marta había querido llorar. _____

5 ¿No habías vuelto a casa? _____

H 3 Put the verb in brackets into the pluperfect tense.

1 Los chicos nunca _____ (*jugar*) al béisbol.

2 Su padre le _____ (*decir*) que iba al trabajo.

3 Y tú, ¿_____ (*ir*) allí antes?

4 Mi amiga y yo ya _____ (*cenar*).

5 Yo _____ (*ver*) la película dos veces.

6 ¿Vosotros _____ (*hacer*) algo interesante?

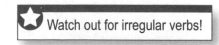

Watch out for irregular verbs!

H 4 **Rewrite these jumbled sentences in the correct order.**

1 trabajado en Manolo allí pasado había el

2 dejado beber habían de alcohol

3 mucho los para escrito habíamos deberes

4 ¿ los puesto habías mesa la libros en ?

5 llegó yo ella había salido cuando

H 5 **Translate these sentences into Spanish.**

1 He had gone to town.

2 They hadn't arrived.

3 I had seen the programme before.

Translate as 'to the town'.

Where do you put the *no*?

Remember that this is irregular.

H 6 **Translate this passage into Spanish.**

Use the preterite.

You don't use *en* here.

When I arrived, Elena had made the evening meal. She had bought all the food on Friday. It had been a good day for me because I had played football and we had won the league. It had been a difficult match and I was very hungry.

Use the imperfect tense. Which verb do you need (not *ser* or *estar*)?

» *Foundation p. 30*
» *Higher pp. 34–35, p. 61, p. 94*

Ⓖ In Spanish, you make sentences negative by adding *no* before the verb.

Salió. He went out. *No salió.* He **didn't** go out.

More specific negatives make a verb 'sandwich', with *no* going before the verb and the rest of the negative expression after the verb.

no … nada	nothing / not … anything / not … at all
no … nadie	no one / not … anyone
no … ni … ni …	neither … nor … / not … either … or
no … ningún / ninguna	not one / not any / not a single
no … nunca	never / not … ever

⭐ Note that *ninguno* becomes *ningún* if used before a masculine singular noun.

No hago *nada*.   I **don't** do **anything**.
No conozco a *nadie*.   I **don't** know **anyone**.
No tenemos *ni* dinero *ni* ideas.   We have **neither** money **nor** ideas.

⭐ Note that *nadie* requires the personal a (see p. 89) before it.

Note that the articles are not used with the negative.

No hay *ningún* problema.   There isn't a single problem.

The 'sandwich' can have quite a generous filling sometimes! You put the following in the middle, between *no* and the rest of the negative:

- all of a compound tense, e.g. the perfect tense: *No* he visto *nada*.   I haven't seen anything.
- all of a verb + infinitive structure: *No* puedo llamar a *nadie*.   I can't call anyone.
- any object pronouns that come before the verb: *Yo no* lo hago *nunca*.   I never do it.

Negatives without *no*

Nunca can also go <u>before</u> the verb. When you use it in this way, *no* isn't needed.

Nunca toma drogas.   She/He **never** takes drugs.
No toma drogas *nunca*.   She/He **never** takes drugs.

Tampoco ('either', 'neither', 'nor' – the negative of *también*) is always used on its own, i.e. without *no*. It goes in front of the verb.

Tampoco hay piscina.   *There isn't a swimming pool either.*

1 **Match the negatives to their English translations.**

1	no … nadie	**a**	neither
2	tampoco	**b**	never
3	nunca	**c**	neither … nor …
4	no … ni … ni …	**d**	not a single
5	no … ningún	**e**	not … anything
6	no … nada	**f**	no one

⭐ In a matching activity, do all the ones you are sure of first – then you will have fewer options to choose from for the more difficult phrases.

2 **Choose the correct negative to complete each sentence.**

1 No descarga *ninguna / nada* aplicación.
2 No tienen billetes. *Tampoco / Ningún* tienen dinero.
3 *No cocinas ni / Nunca cocinas* para tu familia.
4 No ayuda a *nunca / nadie*.
5 No me gustan *ni los caramelos ni el helado / nadie*.
6 No necesitamos *tampoco / nada*.

Think about what follows *me gustan* – singular or plural noun?

3 **Make these sentences negative using the negatives provided.**

> Think about the sandwich filling. See page p. 74.

1 Has ido a España. (*never*) _____

2 Tenía un restaurante y un bar. (*neither … nor*) _____

3 Me chifla una asignatura. (*not a single*) _____

4 Hay espacios verdes. (*neither*) _____

5 Queremos hacer mucho. (*nothing*) _____

6 Oí a una persona. (*no one*) _____

4 **Rewrite these sentences in the correct order, then translate them into English.**

1 gafas Tampoco lleva. _____

_____

2 divertido fue ni ni interesante No. _____

_____

3 nada comer No puedo. _____

_____

4 película Nunca visto esta he. _____

_____

5 **Translate these sentences into Spanish.**

> Refer to the grid on p. 74 for this negative if you are unsure.

1 I don't like pop music at all! _____

_____

2 I never watch TV programmes on my mobile. _____

_____

3 There's neither a cinema nor a hospital in the centre. _____

_____

4 They don't do a single after-school activity. _____

_____

H 6 **Translate this passage into Spanish.**

> Use *quedar bien a.*

In my school, we wear a uniform. Have you seen my jumper? And my shoes? They're really ugly! The uniform isn't nice or comfortable. Nor is it practical. It doesn't suit anyone. I don't like the colours at all. And, in the future, I'm never going to wear a grey skirt again!

> Which negative do you need when you are talking about two things?

> Use *nunca más* for 'never again'.

> Which negative can you use as an intensifier in sentences like this?

_____

_____

_____

_____

_____

G **H** The present subjunctive is a form of the verb which we don't often use in English, but which Spanish speakers use frequently. The subjunctive has certain 'triggers' in Spanish after which it must be used.

One of the key times that the present subjunctive must be used is:

- After *cuando* when talking about the <u>future</u>.
  *Cuando **termine** este curso, <u>buscaré</u> un trabajo.*   When I **finish** this course, <u>I will look for</u> a job.

Spanish speakers instinctively know when to use the subjunctive, but as we don't often use it in English, it can be a challenge to master. Therefore, using it correctly in your GCSE will really impress the examiner and add complexity to your speaking and writing.

To form the present subjunctive, take the first person singular ('I' form) of the present tense, remove the final **–o** and add the following endings:

	gan**ar** (to earn/win)	com**er** (to eat)	viv**ir** (to live)
(yo)	gan**e**	com**a**	viv**a**
(tú)	gan**es**	com**as**	viv**as**
(él/ella/usted)	gan**e**	com**a**	viv**a**
(nosotros/nosotras)	gan**emos**	com**amos**	viv**amos**
(vosotros/vosotras)	gan**éis**	com**áis**	viv**áis**
(ellos/ellas/ustedes)	gan**en**	com**an**	viv**an**

If the first person singular (*yo*) is irregular in the present tense, the subjunctive will take the same form. For example: *tengo* → *tenga*, *hago* → *haga*.

Some verbs are completely irregular in the subjunctive:

ir (to go) → **vaya, vayas, vaya** ...   **ser** (to be) → **sea, seas, sea** ...
dar (to give) → **dé, des, dé** ...   **hay** (there is/are) → **haya**

H 1 **Tick the sentences that would include the present subjunctive if translated into Spanish.**

1 When I finish school, I will take a gap year.   ☐
2 When we go shopping, I always find a bargain!   ☐
3 When you arrive, we will start the film.   ☐
4 When I heard him sing, I almost cried!   ☐

H 2 **There is one mistake in each sentence. Underline the mistake and write the correction above.**

Example: Cuando <u>tengo</u> treinta años, me casaré.   (above: tenga)

1 Compraré un coche cuando gano bastante dinero.

2 Cuando los alumnos terminan sus estudios, irán a Mallorca.

3 Cuando voy de vacaciones, practicaré mi español.

H 3 **Complete the following translations by choosing the correct infinitive from the box and then putting it in the present subjunctive.**

> Remember to use the correct reflexive pronoun before the verb.

> casarse   pasar   ganar   aprobar   ser   perder

1 When I am older...   Cuando .... mayor...
2 When I get married...   Cuando ....
3 When we win the match...   Cuando .... el partido...
4 When I pass my exams...   Cuando .... mis exámenes...

> Stem-changing!

¡Viva! GCSE Spanish © Pearson Education Limited 2017

Verbs Other uses of the present subjunctive

» Higher p. 151, p. 164

(G) Another important time that the present subjunctive must be used is:

(H) • After points of view which use the structure es + adjective + que ...

Es *importante* que ... / Es *esencial* que ... / Es *necesario* que ...

Es *importante* que **ahorremos** energía.   It's important that **we save** energy.

In more general statements when *que* is not used, we use the infinitive instead of the present subjunctive.

Es necesario hacer ejercicio para perder peso. It is necessary to do exercise in order to lose weight.

(For other uses and examples of the present subjunctive, see pp. 234–235 in the Student Book.)

(H) 1 Highlight either the verb in the infinitive or the present subjunctive to complete these sentences.

1 Es muy importante *viajar / viaje* al extranjero una vez en la vida.

2 Es esencial que no *beber / bebas* demasiado alcohol.

3 No es necesario *casarse / se casen* antes de tener hijos hoy en día.

4 Es triste que tantos jóvenes no *tener / tengan* acceso a la educación.

(H) 2 Underline the verbs in the present subjunctive in this passage.

Cuando sea mayor, estudiaré idiomas en la universidad, y por eso es esencial que mejore mi nivel de español. Me gustaría tomarme un año sabático en Honduras. No es justo que haya tantos jóvenes sin techo en ese país, así que cuando llegue, buscaré un trabajo como voluntario en un orfanato.

★ Watch out for verbs that have to change their spelling to retain the correct pronunciation. Can you spot the example here?

(H) 3 Complete the sentences using one of the verbs provided and your own words. Then translate the sentences into English.

tener	hacer	comer	ganar	hay	vivir

1 Para perder peso, es esencial que tú ...

_____

2 Me iré de casa cuando...

_____

3 Es terrible que _____ en el mundo.

_____

Use this pronoun to help you decide which person of the present subjunctive to use.

(H) 4 Translate this passage into Spanish.

Remember that the indefinite article isn't used with occupations in Spanish.

Remember to include the correct definite articles.

I would like to work as a volunteer when I am older. It's not fair that there is so much poverty in our city. Also, I am worried about unemployment and environmental problems. It's essential that we look after the planet and create job opportunities.

A subjunctive 'trigger' can affect more than one verb in a sentence.

_____

_____

_____

_____

Verbs The imperative

>> Higher p. 166

G The imperative is the form of the verb that is used to give commands and instructions.

There are positive commands ('Put your hand up!') and negative commands ('Don't shout out!'). These are formed differently depending not only on whether they are positive or negative, but also on the person they are directed at.

Positive commands:

For one person (*tú*), remove the final *–s* from the *tú* form of the verb.

hablar → (tú) hablas → ¡Habla!	Speak! (you singular)
beber → (tú) bebes → ¡Bebe!	Drink! (you singular)

These verbs are irregular in the *tú* form of the imperative:

decir (to say) → **di**	*salir* (to go/get out) → **sal**
hacer (to do/make) → **haz**	*ser* (to be) → **sé**
ir (to go) → **ve**	*tener* (to have) → **ten**
poner (to put) → **pon**	*venir* (to come) → **ven**

For more than one person (*vosotros/vosotras*), change the final *–r* of the infinitive to *–d*.

escribir → ¡Escribid!	Write! (you plural)

H For formal positive commands, use the present subjunctive (see p. 76).

comer → ¡Coma!	Eat! (you singular formal)
comprar → ¡Compren!	Buy! (you plural formal)

⭐ Watch out for spelling changes in the present subjunctive that are needed to keep the same pronunciation.
apa**gar** (to switch off) → apa**gue**
prote**ger** (to protect) → prote**ja**
utili**jar** (to use) → utili**ce**

H **Negative commands:**

For all negative commands, use the present subjunctive (see p. 76).

gritar → ¡No grites!	Don't shout!	(you singular)
reciclar → ¡No recicle!	Don't recycle!	(you singular formal)
coger → ¡No cojáis!	Don't take!	(you plural)
subir → ¡No suban!	Don't go up!	(you plural formal)

---

1 Match the Spanish and English sentences.

1	¡No comas chicle!	a Wait for your turn to speak.
2	Sea puntual.	b Don't chew chewing gum!
3	Respeta el turno de palabra.	c Keep the playground clean.
4	¡No corráis en los pasillos!	d Be on time.
5	Mantén limpio el patio.	e Don't run in the corridors!

⭐ Remember in English we only have one way of saying 'you', whereas in Spanish there are several options: *tú* (informal singular); *usted* (formal singular); *vosotros/vosotras* (informal plural); *ustedes* (formal plural).

2 Put the verb in brackets into the correct form of the imperative.

1 _____ (*separar, tú*) la basura.

2 _____ (*plantar, vosotros*) más árboles.

3 _____ (*usar, tú*) menos agua.

H 4 No _____ (*malgastar, tú*) energía.

H 5 _____ (*apagar, ustedes*) los aparatos eléctricos.

H 6 No _____ (*ir, tú*) en coche todos los días.

⭐ Remember that the 'you formal singular' (*usted*) form of the verb uses the same endings as the 'he/she/it' form and the 'you formal plural' (*ustedes*) form uses the same endings as the 'they' form of the verb.

Think about how we keep the pronunciation of *apa**gar***.

This is irregular in the present subjunctive.

3 Translate the first three sentences from exercise 2 into English.

1 ....

2 ....

3 ....

4 Read the following statements and then give an appropriate piece of advice using the imperative in the *tú* (you singular) form.

Example: No desenchufo la televisión. Desenchufa la televisión.

1 No como fruta.

....

2 No reciclo ni papel ni vidrio.

....

(H) 3 Tiro basura al suelo.

....

(H) 4 Consumo mucha energía.
| Change this to 'so much' in your piece of advice. |

....

5 Using the verb in brackets and the appropriate form of the imperative, translate these sentences into Spanish.

1 Eat an apple every day. (*comer – vosotros*)

....

2 Look after your brother, please. (*cuidar – tú*)
| Remember to include the personal *a* after this verb. |

....

(H) 3 Don't send messages in class. (*mandar – tú*)

....

(H) 4 Don't go by car, take the bus. (*ir, coger – ustedes*)
| Think about how we keep the pronunciation of *coger*. |

....

6 Translate this passage into Spanish. Use either *tú* or *usted* for 'you' throughout the whole passage, as it should all be directed at the same person.

| Here you need to use *tener que*. | | Here you need to use *llevar*. |

We have to save the planet! Don't be lazy! Live a greener life! Recycle paper and don't throw rubbish on the ground! The air is polluted so reduce vehicle emissions and go to school by bike. There is too much deforestation so don't cut down so many trees and plant more woods!

| Use *así que* here. | | Remember to use *en* when travelling 'by' something. |

....

....

....

....

....

G The imperfect subjunctive is the past tense equivalent of the present subjunctive; a form of the verb which
H we don't often use in English but which is used a lot in Spanish.

The imperfect subjunctive is most commonly used in 'if' clauses that are followed by a verb in
the underlined conditional.

> Si **fuera** rico, (compraría) un Ferrari.   If **I were** rich, I would buy a Ferrari.
>
> Si **pudieras** tomarte un año sabático, ¿te gustaría trabajar como voluntario?
> If **you could** take a gap year, would you like to work as a volunteer?
>
> Si **tuviéramos** más tiempo, pasaríamos una semana allí.
> If **we had** more time, we would spend a week there.

> [imperfect subjunctive]
>
> [conditional]

> ⭐ See pp. 64–65 to remind you how to form the conditional.

Using sentences like these that include the imperfect subjunctive will add complexity and grammatical variety
to your speaking and writing. You may also need to be able to recognise the imperfect subjunctive to fully
understand a spoken or written text.

To form the imperfect subjunctive, take the third person plural of the
preterite (e.g. *hicieron* – they made/did, *jugaron* – they played), remove
the final **–ron** and add these endings:

> ⭐ See pp. 50–55 to remind you how to form the preterite.

	ganar (to earn/win)	**beber** (to drink)	**vivir** (to live)
(yo)	gana**ra**	bebie**ra**	vivie**ra**
(tú)	gana**ras**	bebie**ras**	vivie**ras**
(él/ella/usted)	gana**ra**	bebie**ra**	vivie**ra**
(nosotros/nosotras)	ganá**ramos**	bebié**ramos**	vivié**ramos**
(vosotros/vosotras)	gana**rais**	bebie**reis**	vivie**reis**
(ellos/ellas/ustedes)	gana**ran**	bebie**ran**	vivie**ran**

If the third person plural (*ellos/ellas*) of the preterite is irregular, the imperfect subjunctive will take the same form:

> tener (to have) → tuvie~~ron~~ → tuvie**ra**
> ir/ser (to go/to be) → fue~~ron~~ → fue**ra**

H 1 Tick the sentences that would include the imperfect subjunctive if translated into Spanish.

1 If you study hard, you will pass your exams. ☐
2 If I worked for a charity, I would like it to be abroad. ☐
3 If they looked harder, they would find the answer. ☐
4 You wouldn't win a single game if you played against me! ☐
5 If you listen to the teacher, you will make more progress! ☐
6 Wouldn't it be nice if we went on holiday? ☐

H 2 Match the Spanish and English phrases.

1 Si ganara...   a If I could...
2 Si viajara...   b If I had...
3 Si pudiera...   c If I were/went...
4 Si hiciera...   d If I won/earned...
5 Si tuviera...   e If I travelled...
6 Si fuera...   f If I did/made...

> ⭐ Ask yourself which verbs look similar in the third person plural (they form) of the preterite tense.

H 3 Complete these sentences with the correct verb from the box in the 'I' form of the imperfect subjunctive.

> ir   hacer   ganar   poder   ser   viajar   tener

1 Si _____ la lotería, compraría un apartamento en Sevilla.

2 Si _____ a Perú, visitaría Machu Picchu.

3 Si _____ más deportista, aprendería a esquiar.

4 Si _____ los deberes, mi profesor estaría contento.

5 Si _____ a la universidad, estudiaría medicina.

> ⭐ Remember that *ser* and *ir* are the same in the preterite and therefore the same in the imperfect subjunctive.

H 4 Unjumble these sentences and then translate them into English.

> ⭐ Remember that the conditional comes after the imperfect subjunctive.

1 dinero, bastante Si un Argentina. tuviera año pasaría en

_____

_____

> ⭐ Use the punctuation to help you!

2 vivieras español. mejorarías Si nivel España, en tu de

_____

_____

3 más fuéramos Si mochila con mundo. viajaríamos independientes, por el

_____

_____

_____

H 5 Complete these translations into Spanish.

> ⭐ Look carefully at the person of the verb!

1 If I had a younger brother, I would get on well with him.

_____ un hermano menor, me llevaría bien con él.

> ⭐ See p. 64 on how to conjugate the conditional.

2 If we studied more, we would get good marks!

¡_____ más, sacaríamos buenas notas!

3 If they were more sociable, they would make new friends.

_____ más sociables, harían nuevos amigos.

4 If I won the lottery, I would help to build a school

_____, _____ a construir un colegio.

> Use *tomarnos* here.

5 If we could take a gap year, we would support an environmental project.

_____

> *Poder* is irregular in the conditional.

6 If you (singular) had more time in Barcelona, you would be able to visit Park Güell.

_____

Verbs The passive voice

>> Higher p. 121

G
H The passive is used to describe what action is/was/will be done to something or someone. The **object** becomes the <u>subject</u> of the sentence.

<u>My friend</u> took **the photo**. → <u>The photo</u> was taken by **my friend**.
*<u>Mi amigo</u> sacó **la foto**. → <u>La foto</u> fue sacada por **mi amigo**.*

You may want to use the passive when describing an event and you will need to be able to understand it in spoken and written texts.

To form the passive, use the correct person and tense of **ser** followed by the <u>past participle</u>, which must agree in number and gender with the object.

*La Sagrada Familia **fue** <u>diseñada</u> por Gaudí.*
The Sagrada Familia **was** <u>designed</u> by Gaudí.

*Durante el festival, las casas **son** <u>decoradas</u> con flores.*
During the festival, the houses **are** <u>decorated</u> with flowers.

Watch out for verbs that are irregular in the past participle:

hacer → hecho   escribir → escrito   ver → visto   decir → dicho

(See p. 70 on how to form the past participle.)

H 1 Complete these sentences by adding the correct form of *ser* and the correct past participle from the boxes.

ser	
es	fue
son	serán
será	fueron

Past participles			
disparadas	escrito	ganada	ganado
pintado	disparados	hablada	escrito
escritas	hablado	pintada	ganados

1 The painting *Guernica* was painted by Picasso.

El cuadro *Guernica* _____ por Picasso.

2 The fireworks are set off at midnight.

Los fuegos artificiales _____ a medianoche.

3 The Harry Potter books were written by J.K. Rowling.

Las novelas de Harry Potter _____ por J.K. Rowling.

4 The Champions League will be won by a Spanish team.

La Liga de Campeones _____ por un equipo español.

5 Spanish is spoken by more than 450 million people.

El español _____ por más de 450 millones de personas.

> ⭐ Remember to choose the correct person and tense of *ser* and that the past participle must agree with the object.

H 2 Translate these sentences into English.

> Remember that *de* can mean 'of' or 'from' depending on the context of the sentence.

1 Millones de tomates son exportados de Andalucía cada año.

_____

2 El gazpacho fue inventado en España.

_____

3 Mi instituto fue construido hace 150 años.

_____

Verbs Avoiding the passive

» Higher p. 122

> **G** The passive is not used as much in Spanish as it is in English. In fact, when it is not clear who or what has
> **H** done the action, Spanish speakers prefer to avoid the passive.
>
> You do this by using the pronoun **se** with the third person singular or plural of the verb.
>
> | | |
> |---|---|
> | **Se celebra** *la fiesta.* | The festival **is celebrated**. |
> | **Se construyen** *hogueras.* | Bonfires **are built**. |
>
> It is most common when the identity of the person who carries out the action isn't important. In English, we
> sometimes use 'you' or 'one' in these sentences.
>
> | | |
> |---|---|
> | **Se puede** *ver el desfile.* | **You/One can** see the procession. |
> | No **se debe** *comer chicle.* | **You/One must** not chew chewing gum. |

**H 1 Read the following text about Madrid's San Isidro festival and underline all nine examples of
passive avoidance.**

> Men wearing giant papier-mâché heads!

> This is a traditional dance from Madrid.

Las fiestas de San Isidro se celebran en mayo en Madrid y el evento se repite cada año. Las calles, donde se
puede ver el desfile de *los Cabezudos*, se llenan de gente. Se escucha música tradicional y se baila el chotis.
En el parque se hace un picnic enorme donde se come la comida madrileña tradicional. También, se
disparan muchos fuegos artificiales por la noche.

H 2 Use an appropriate verb from the box with the pronoun *se* to complete these translations.

poder	hablar	necesitar	lanzar	comer	celebrar

1 The festival is celebrated in May. _____ la fiesta en mayo.

> ⭐ Remember to use the third person singular (he/she/it) or plural (they) form of the verb.

2 You can see a procession. _____ ver un desfile.

3 Portuguese is spoken in Brazil. _____ portugués en Brasil.

4 Tomatoes are thrown. _____ tomates.

5 You need sunglasses. _____ gafas de sol.

> Think: is the noun singular or plural?

H 3 Translate this passage into Spanish.

> Use *de* here.

Glastonbury is my favourite festival in England. It is celebrated every year in June. The fields are filled with
young people, music and tents. It is a place where new artists are discovered and new friends are made.

> In Spanish, this word is the same as 'shops'.

_____

_____

_____

_____

¡Viva! GCSE Spanish © Pearson Education Limited 2017

83

G Desde hace + present tense

You can use *hace* to talk about a time in the past.

hace dos años   two years **ago**   *hace* un mes   a month **ago**

To say in Spanish how long you've been doing something, you use *desde hace* and the **present tense** of the verb.

¿Desde hace cuánto tiempo **tocas** el piano?   How long have you been playing the piano?
Toco el piano *desde hace* cinco años.   I've been playing the piano for five years.

You can use *desde hace* with lots of time phrases, such as *minutos* (minutes), *días* (days), *semanas* (weeks), *meses* (months), *años* (years).

H Desde hacía + imperfect tense

To say how long something <u>had been happening</u> when an event occurred, you use *desde hacía* (*hacía* is the imperfect tense of *hacer* – for more details on the imperfect, see pp. 56–57).

Esperábamos desde hacía una hora cuando llegó.   We had been waiting for an hour when he arrived.

Note that the verb describing what you were doing before the event occurred is in the imperfect tense, too.

Trabajaba en la tienda desde hacía cuatro   I had been working in the shop for four months
meses cuando conocí a Jorge.   when I met Jorge.

⭐ Work out what kind of word the next word in the sentence needs to be. This will help you find the correct ending.

1 Match these sentence halves.

1 Leo tebeos desde hace   a tiempo quieres ir a Francia?

2 Trabajan de dependientes desde   b cuánto tiempo asistes a este insti?

3 ¿Desde hace   c cuatro meses.

4 Tengo este ordenador   d hace un año.

5 ¿Desde   e hace cuánto tiempo juegas al fútbol?

6 ¿Desde hace cuánto   f desde hace tres semanas.

2 Rewrite these sentences in the correct order. Then write the sentence numbers in order from the shortest time described to the longest.

Look for the verb to get you started.

1 judo desde hace días practicamos diez. ....

2 minutos desde hace cocino quince. ....

3 toco la desde seis meses hace guitarra. ....

4 hace senderismo año desde hacen un. ....

5 una hace ves la película de desde hora terror. ....

6 más de desde un año voluntario soy hace. ....

Shortest time to longest time: ☐ ☐ ☐ ☐ ☐ ☐

H 3 Complete the sentences with the correct form of the verb in brackets and any other missing words.

1 _____ (*ir, yo*) al parque desde _____ dos semanas.

2 _____ (*sacar, él*) fotos _____ hace ocho meses.

3 ¿Desde hace _____ tiempo la _____ (*tener, tú*)?

4 _____ (*conocerse, nosotros*) _____ hace tres años.

5 ¿Desde hace cuánto _____ _____ (*hacer, vosotros*) karting?

6 _____ (*ayudar, ellos*) a los clientes desde _____ dos años.

> What tense do you need to use with *desde hace*?

4 Choose four endings to the question, using the ideas supplied. Then answer the questions in Spanish giving your own response and translate your answers into English.

> ¿Desde hace cuánto tiempo …

> vas al …?   tocas …?   tienes …?   haces …?
> practicas …?   juegas al …?   estudias …?

1 _____
_____

2 _____
_____

3 _____
_____

4 _____
_____

H 5 Translate these sentences into Spanish.

> Think carefully about which tense you use here.

1 Mateo has had a mobile for three months. _____

2 There has been a museum here for 100 years. _____

3 We've been staying in the youth hostel for a week. _____

H 6 Translate this passage into Spanish.

> Which tense in Spanish?

I've loved music for many years. I've played the guitar for four years and my friend Ben has played it for more than two years – and now we're members of a band! The band's called The Crazy Rabbits. We'd been giving concerts for six months when we decided to choose that name. How long have you played an instrument?

> Don't be put off – you still need the imperfect here.

_____
_____
_____
_____

(G) A preposition is a word or phrase that shows the relationship of one thing to another. They often tell you <u>where</u> something is in relation to something else:

> *La tienda está **al lado del** museo.*   The shop is **next to** the museum.
> *El museo está **delante de** la tienda.*   The museum is **in front of** the shop.

Prepositions are useful words for adding detail to your speaking or writing.
Here are some common prepositions:

a	to	*delante de*	in front of
de	from, of	*dentro de*	inside
a la derecha de	to the right of	*detrás de*	behind
a la izquierda de	to the left of	*en*	in, on, at
al final de	at the end of	*encima de*	on (top of)
al lado de	next to	*enfrente de*	opposite
debajo de	under	*entre … y …*	between … and …

You need to think carefully about the gender of the noun that follows your preposition:

a + el → al
masculine: *Voy **al** parque.*   I'm going **to the** park.
feminine: *Voy **a la** bolera.*   I'm going **to the** bowling alley.

de + el → del
masculine: *delante **del** cine*   in front **of the** cinema
feminine: *delante **de la** piscina* in front **of the** swimming pool

---

1 **Complete the sentences with *al, a la, a los, a las, del, de la, de los* or *de las*.**

⭐ Look carefully at the last word in each sentence.

1 ¿Para ir _____ playa?

2 Está dentro _____ polideportivo.

3 Voy _____ teatro.

4 Estoy enfrente _____ iglesia.

5 Está al lado _____ bares.

6 Vamos _____ tiendas.

2 **Write the words from the box in the correct order by following the Spanish instructions.**

⭐ This sentence includes a Spanish saying; an expression that can't be translated literally. You can find the meaning in the answers section of this book.

española	es	La	comido	gramática	pan

La palabra 'gramática' está a la izquierda de 'española' y 'comido' está al final de la frase; 'pan' está al lado de 'comido' pero a la derecha de 'es'. Finalmente, 'La' está delante de 'gramática'.

---

3 **Translate these sentences into Spanish.**

1 The shop is to the right of the library.

Because we are talking about location here, you need to use *está* and not *es*.

_____

2 The market is opposite the town hall.

_____

You need the preterite here.

3 Yesterday I went to the cinema which is next to the ice rink.

Use *que* here.

_____

(G) *Por* and *para* can both be translated as 'for', however they nearly always have different meanings in a sentence.

Trabajo **por** ellos.	I work **for** them. (ie. for their benefit)
Trabajo **para** ellos.	I work **for** them. (ie. they employ me)

Just one word can make a big difference to the meaning of a sentence, therefore it is important to learn which of these prepositions to use. This will improve the accuracy of your spoken and written work and will help you fully understand listening and reading texts.

Por

We use *por* when we want to say **for** (<u>the benefit of</u>) or <u>because of</u>:

Ahorro energía **por** el medio ambiente	I save energy **for** (the benefit of) the environment.
No podemos salir **por** la lluvia.	We can't go out because of the rain.

Para

We use *para* when we want to say **for** a <u>person</u>, <u>destination</u> or <u>purpose</u>:

Compré este regalo **para** <u>mi amigo</u>.	I bought this present **for** <u>my friend</u>.
El tren sale **para** <u>Barcelona</u>.	The train is leaving **for** <u>Barcelona</u>.
¿**Para** <u>qué</u> quieres el dinero?	<u>What</u> do you want the money **for**?

In Spanish, you must never end a sentence with a preposition, even though this is common in English.

Other uses

Por can also be used when talking about <u>when something happens</u> or it can mean **by** (someone/something):

Salgo con mis amigos <u>**por** la noche</u>.	I go out with my friends <u>at night</u>.
Fue escrito **por** Suzanne Collins.	It was written **by** Suzanne Collins.

Para can also mean **for** when expressing a <u>time limit</u>.
Los deberes son **para** <u>el jueves</u>.	The homework is **for** <u>Thursday</u>.

1 Complete the sentences with either *por* or *para*.

1   She bought the ticket for me.   *Compró la entrada _____ mí.*

2   I did it for her benefit.   *Lo hice _____ ella.*

3   The bus is leaving for Bilbao.   *El autobús sale _____ Bilbao.*

4   Thank you for the present   *Gracias _____ el regalo.*

5   I am stressed because of exams.   *Estoy estresado _____ los exámenes.*

2 Translate these sentences into Spanish.

1   The bus for Valladolid left ten minutes ago.

_____

2   I admire Ed Sheeran for his attitude.

> Here you need to use the personal 'a'.

_____

3   A tea for me, thank you.

_____

4   I run for my health.

> ⭐ Ask yourself if 'for' can be replaced by 'for the benefit of' or 'because of'.

_____

5   I work as a volunteer for the homeless.

_____

Prepositions Expressions with infinitives

(G) There are certain expressions in Spanish that are followed by the <u>infinitive</u> ('to do' something) even though often, when translated into English, we use the <u>present participle</u> (the '–ing' form).

Antes de <u>llegar</u> al festival …   **Before** <u>arriving</u> at the festival …

Using a range of these expressions will add complexity and variety to your spoken and written work.

Here are some common expressions followed by infinitives:

- **antes de** + <u>infinitive</u>   before (doing)
  Antes de <u>acostarme</u>, me ducho.   **Before** going to bed, I shower.
- **después de** + <u>infinitive</u>   after (doing)
  Después de <u>cenar</u>, salí.   **After** eating dinner, I went out.
- (H) **al** + <u>infinitive</u>   on (doing)
  Al <u>ver</u> a mi amigo, sonreí.   **On** seeing my friend, I smiled.
- (H) **sin** + <u>infinitive</u>   without (doing)
  Pasé dos noches **sin** <u>dormir</u>.   I spent two nights **without** sleeping.

The following expressions take the infinitive (but not always the present participle in the English translation).

- **para** + <u>infinitive</u>   in order to (do)/for –ing
  Uso YouTube **para** <u>ver</u> vídeos.   I use YouTube **in order to** watch videos.
- **acabar de** + <u>infinitive</u>   to have just (done)
  ¡**Acabo de** <u>ver</u> a Sam Smith!   I **have just** seen Sam Smith!
- **tener ganas de** + <u>infinitive</u>   to fancy/feel like (doing)
  (H) **Tengo ganas de** <u>ir</u> al cine.   I **fancy** going to the cinema.

Acabar de and **tener ganas de** can be used in different tenses and cannot be translated word for word.

- **Acababa de** levantarme.   I **had just** got up.
  Tendré ganas de salir más tarde.   I **will feel like** going out later.

1 **Write which expression you would need if translating the following phrases into Spanish.**

Example: **On** arriving home … Al

1 **He has just** finished … _____
2 **Before** getting up … _____
(H) 3 **I don't fancy** going. _____
(H) 4 **Without** knowing it … _____

> Remember that you need the correct person of the verb for these expressions.

2 **Translate these sentences into English.**

1 Acabamos de volver de un festival.

_____

2 Uso Spotify para escuchar música.

_____

3 Después de cenar, hago los deberes.

_____

> You will need three words in English.

3 **Translate these sentences into Spanish.**

1 I have just arrived at Glastonbury.

_____

2 Before seeing Coldplay, I am going to see Pharrell Williams.

_____

(H) 3 Last year, my friend spent four days without sleeping.

_____

> Remember this cannot be translated word for word.

> You will need the near future tense here.

> You will need the preterite here.

Prepositions   The personal *a*

> **G** When the object of the verb is a known person or pet animal, you must always place *a* immediately before it.
> **H** This is called the personal *a*.
>
> Vi **a** mi ⟨amigo⟩ Sebastián.   I saw my friend Sebastián.
> Va a visitar **a** su abuela.   He is going to visit his grandmother.
>
> verb
> object
>
> As the personal *a* doesn't exist in English, it is a detail we often miss when learning Spanish. However, understanding when it is needed and using it appropriately is essential in order to make your spoken and written work accurate.
>
> You do <u>not</u> use the personal *a* when the person (or animal) is someone you cannot picture or do not know. Compare these two sentences for example:
>
> Busco **a** mi perro.   I'm looking for **my** dog.   Busco un perro.   I'm looking for **a** dog.
>
> Remember, if the noun that follows the personal *a* is masculine and takes the definite article (*el*), you must write *al*.
>
> Ayudé **al** profesor en la clase.   I helped the teacher in class.
>
> Note that the personal *a* is not used directly after the verb *tener*.

1 Which sentences need the personal *a*? Add *a* where it is needed.

Example: Veo ^a mis sobrinos una vez al mes.
                I see my nephews once a month.

1   Conoció su mejor amiga hace cinco años.
    She met her best friend five years ago.

2   Busco un novio que me acepte como soy.
    I'm looking for a boyfriend who accepts me as I am.

3   Los sábados mi hermano y yo paseamos el perro en el parque.
    On Saturdays my brother and I walk the dog in the park.

> Remember: *a* + *el* becomes *al*.

2 Translate these sentences into Spanish.

1   I help my brother with his homework.

> You need *sus* here because 'homework' is plural in Spanish.

_____

2   I saw Imagine Dragons at Leeds Fest.

> Use *en* here.

_____

3   They visit their stepfather once a week.

_____

H 3 Translate this passage into Spanish.

> The personal *a* must come before every object of the verb in a sentence.

Yesterday I went to my primary school which is next to the church. I saw my teacher and my little brother. I have to look after my brother every day. Normally we visit our uncle in his shop which is opposite the park.

> Is 'park' masculine or feminine?

_____

_____

_____

Connectives

» Foundation p. 55
» Higher p. 59

(G) Connectives, or conjunctions, are words like 'and', 'but', 'also', 'therefore', and 'because'.

Using connectives will allow you to create extended sentences and give structure to your spoken and written work. Learning them will also help you to fully understand listening and reading texts.

Connectives link sentences or parts of sentences together.

*Le encanta la biología **pero** odia la física.*   She loves biology **but** she hates physics.

*Leo blogs cada día **porque** son gratis, **y también** leo periódicos.*
I read blogs every day **because** they are free, **and** I **also** read newspapers.

Remember that **y** changes to **e** if it comes before a word beginning with *i*– or *hi*– and **o** changes to **u** before words beginning with *o*– or *ho*–.

*Mi profesor es severo **e** impaciente.*   My teacher is harsh **and** impatient.
*¿Para siete **u** ocho noches?*   For seven **or** eight nights?

Here are some useful connectives:

Introduction/Sequence		Justification	
primero	first		
segundo	second	*porque*	because
luego/entonces	then	*ya que*	as, since
más tarde	later	*dado que*	given that
antes (de)	before	*puesto que*	since
después (de)	after		
finalmente	finally		
Addition		**Consequence**	
además	also, as well	*para*	in order to
también	also	*así que*	so, therefore
y/e	and	*por eso*	therefore
o/u	or	*por lo tanto*	therefore
Opposition		**Conclusion**	
aunque	although		
mientras que	while/whereas	*en resumen*	to sum up
pero	but	*en conclusión*	in conclusion
por otro lado	on the other hand		
sin embargo	however		

(For more examples of connectives, see p. 229 in the Higher Student Book or p. 215 in the Foundation Student Book.)

1 Match up the Spanish and English phrases.

1	ya que me interesa el deporte	a	then I get dressed
2	mientras que era animado	b	as sport interests me
3	además la ducha está sucia	c	therefore I prefer languages
4	luego me visto	d	the shower is dirty as well
5	por eso prefiero los idiomas	e	while it used to be lively

2 Fill in the gaps with a suitable connective from the box.

1 Mi instituto tiene un campo de fútbol _____ no tiene gimnasio.

2 Me gusta leer tebeos _____ ver películas.

3 Mi hermano estudia música _____ le encanta tocar el piano.

4 El sábado compré recuerdos y _____ fui al acuario.

5 Tenemos cinco _____ seis clases al día.

> y
> después
> pero
> o
> ya que

3 Match up the sentence halves.

1 Prefiero ir a la costa …
2 Hay que ser puntual, …
3 Escuchan música …
4 A menudo lee revistas, …
5 Primero me lavo los dientes, …

a mientras hacen los deberes.
b sin embargo nunca lee novelas.
c luego me visto.
d aunque siempre llego tarde.
e puesto que me encanta bucear.

4 Translate these sentences into English.

> Don't include this word in your translation.

1 Mi día preferido es el martes porque estudio historia.

....

2 Mi insti es antiguo, sin embargo tiene unos laboratorios modernos.

....

3 Uso Snapchat para mandar fotos, por otro lado uso WhatsApp para mandar mensajes.

> This can be translated as 'in order to' or 'for –ing'.

....

....

5 Translate these sentences into Spanish.

1 On Mondays, first I have maths and then I have PE.

....

2 It's a funny book; it's very interesting as well.

> Don't put this connective at the end of your translation.

....

3 Normally I go by bus although sometimes I go on foot.

> We use *en* when we go by a vehicle. What do we use when we go on foot?

....

H 6 Translate this passage into Spanish.

> Remember, when following opinion phrases, nouns always need their definite article.

> The next word begins with *i*– when translated. How will this affect the connective?

I love languages and therefore I study Spanish, French and English. Every day I read a magazine or a newspaper. Also, I use my mobile to read blogs and download books, although I prefer a traditional book. On the other hand, e-books are cheaper.

> You need *para* here.

> Remember, there isn't one word in Spanish for 'cheaper'. You need to say 'more cheap'.

....

....

....

....

....

....

Combining tenses Preterite, present and near future

G At GCSE, it is very important to demonstrate that you can use a range of tenses, as it adds complexity and variety to your spoken and written work.

Use the **preterite** to say what someone <u>did</u>. It is used for completed actions in the past:

    Comió *una pizza.*   **He ate** a pizza.

Use the **present tense** to say what <u>usually</u> happens, what things <u>are</u> like and what is happening <u>now</u>:

    *Normalmente **juego** al rugby.*   Normally **I play** rugby.
    *La novela **es** interesante.*   The novel **is** interesting.

Use the **near future tense** to say what <u>is going to</u> happen:

    Vas a trabajar *duro.*   **You are going to work** hard.

Spotting time phrases can often help you identify whether someone is referring to the past, present or future. Using them will add context and detail to your spoken and written work.

Here are some common time phrases:

past	present	future
ayer yesterday	*normalmente* normally	*mañana* tomorrow
anteayer/antes de ayer the day before yesterday	*en general/generalmente* in general/generally	*pasado mañana* the day after tomorrow
anoche last night	*en este momento* at the moment	*esta noche* tonight
la semana pasada last week	*ahora* now	*la semana que viene* next week
el mes pasado last month	*hoy en día* nowadays	*el mes que viene* next month
el año pasado last year	*actualmente* currently/nowadays	*el año que viene* next year

> ★ To remind yourself how to form the tenses, see pp. 50–55 for the preterite, pp. 36–41 for the present tense and pp. 60–61 for the near future tense.

Note that ***hoy*** (today) could be used with all three tenses, so understanding context is important.

<u>Normalmente</u> los sábados hago natación (pero) *hoy **jugué** al golf.*
También por la noche <u>suelo</u> salir con mis amigos, (sin embargo)
hoy voy a visitar *a mi abuela.*

> In this passage, these connectives indicate a change from what <u>normally</u> happens or <u>tends to</u> happen to what happened on a particular occasion.

<u>Normally</u> on Saturday I go swimming but **today I played** golf. Also in the evening <u>I tend to</u> go out with my friends, however **today I am going to visit** my grandmother.

1 **Which tenses are used in these sentences: preterite (P), present (PR) or near future (NF)?**

  1 Mañana voy a visitar a mis amigos. ....

  2 Anoche fuimos al cine. ....

  3 Generalmente leen una hora al día. ....

  4 Mi hermano es molesto. ....

  5 El fin de semana pasado hice equitación. ....

2 **Find the verbs in the passage and highlight them using a different colour for each tense. Fill in the key with your chosen colours.**

> Normalmente salgo de casa a las siete pero hoy me desperté tarde y salí a las ocho. El día escolar es muy largo y aburrido pero mañana voy a ir de excursión con mi clase de geografía. ¡Va a ser genial!

☐ pret.
☐ pres.
☐ near fut.

¡Viva! GCSE Spanish © Pearson Education Limited 2017

3 **Look at Leandro's diary and complete his description of his half term holiday by putting the verbs in brackets into the correct person and tense.**

Normalmente .... (*ir*) al insti durante la semana, pero

ahora ¡............................ (*estar*) de vacaciones! Anteayer fui al parque

y .... (*jugar*) al fútbol con Javier. Ayer mi hermano y yo

.... (*visitar*) a nuestros padres y cenamos con ellos.

Esta noche .... (*ir*) a un concierto en el estadio.

¡............................ (*ser*) guay! Mañana .... (*ver*) la nueva película

de James Bond con mi novia, Ana. Pasado mañana es su cumpleaños y

.... (*comprar*) un regalo especial para ella. Este fin de semana

.... (*hacer*) los deberes. ¡Qué rollo!

> **lunes**
> – fútbol
> **martes**
> – padres con hermano
> **miércoles**
> – ¡concierto!
> **jueves**
> – cine, James Bond
> **viernes**
> – cumple de Ana
> **sábado/domingo**
> – deberes 🙁

⭐ Look at the time phrases to help you decide which tense to use.

4 **Translate these sentences into English.**

1 Ayer llovió y hoy hay tormenta pero mañana va a hacer sol.

....

2 Normalmente cenamos en casa pero esta noche vamos a ir a un restaurante.

....

3 Anoche salí con mis amigos así que hoy tengo que cuidar a mi hermano.

....

⭐ Think carefully about which tense you need to use. Look back at the relevant grammar pages to remind you how to form each tense.

5 **Translate these sentences into Spanish.**

1 Yesterday I went horse riding but today I am going to go swimming.

....

2 Now she studies geography but next year she is going to study history.

....

3 We are going to visit my brother in France because at the moment he lives in Paris.

....

ⓗ 6 **Translate this passage into Spanish.** | You need the definite article here. |

Sunday was my birthday but I opened my presents today because my dad arrived home this morning. He works hard and is very generous. Tonight we are going to go to the cinema and it is going to be lots of fun.

| a + el → ? | | you need the word for 'very' here. |

....

....

....

....

Combining tenses   Using past tenses together correctly

» Higher p. 85

G
H
Often when talking about something in the past, we will naturally want to use more than one of the past tenses. Being able to use the different past tenses together correctly can be impressive and create complex pieces of work.

Use the **imperfect tense** to say what someone <u>used to do</u>, or to describe things in the past.

Hacía gimnasia.	**She used to do** gymnastics.
Tenía 12 años.	**He was** 12 years old.

Use the **preterite tense** to say what someone <u>did</u>.

Participó en un torneo.	**She participated** in a tournament.

Use the **perfect tense** to say what someone <u>has done</u>.

Ha batido varios récords.	**He has broken** various records.

Should you need a reminder on how to form each of these tenses, look back at pp. 50–55 for the preterite, pp. 56–57 for the imperfect tense and pp. 70–71 for the perfect tense. Alternatively, refer to the verb tables on pp. 124–128.

H 1 **Match the Spanish and English sentences.**

1	He trabajado muy duro.		a	They made me laugh.
2	Eras pensativo y fiel.		b	I have worked very hard.
3	Cantábamos en un grupo.		c	You were thoughtful and loyal.
4	Ganó una medalla de oro.		d	We used to sing in a group.
5	Me hicieron reír.		e	She won a gold medal.

H 2 **Identify the tense of the verbs in these sentences: imperfect, preterite or perfect?**

1   ¡Mis hermanos han comido toda la pizza sin dejarme un trozo! _____

2   Mi padre conducía cuando ocurrió el accidente. _____   _____

3   Te vi ayer en el autobús. ¿Adónde ibas? _____   _____

4   Nuestra amiga Alba ha comprado las entradas para el cine. _____

5   ¿Hablasteis con vuestro profesor ayer? _____

6   Cuando vivíamos en Barcelona, hablábamos catalán. _____   _____

H 3 **Complete these sentences with the correct person and tense of the verb in brackets.**

1   ¡ _____ (*comer*, *vosotros*, preterite) mi última chocolatina!

2   De pequeño, _____ (*ser*, *yo*, imperfect) muy travieso. | Irregular in the imperfect tense! |

3   Antes de ser ciclista _____ (*jugar*, *ella*, imperfect) al fútbol.

4   _____ (*ver*, *nosotros*, perfect) todas sus películas. | Irregular as a past participle! |

5   En el aeropuerto _____ (*perder*, *ellos*, preterite) su equipaje.

6   _____ (*ganar*, *tú*, perfect) bastante dinero para comprar un nuevo coche.

4 Translate these sentences into English.

1 Cuando era más joven me gustaba hacer atletismo.

2 Cuando vivíamos en Londres participamos en el maratón.

3 No hiciste los deberes así que has copiado el trabajo de tu amigo.

4 Nunca he tenido novio, ¡pero ayer salí con Santi y fue muy divertido!

H 5 Translate these sentences into Spanish.

1 We used to have a motorbike but last year we bought a car.

2 He has suffered various injuries but last summer he won the tournament.

3 The hotel didn't have a bar so we had to go to the city centre.

> We don't need the indefinite article if it follows a negative.

> You should use *tener que* here.

H 6 Translate this passage into Spanish.

> Use *desde que* here.

> Which verb do we use when talking about age?

> ⭐ • Look carefully for clues like time phrases when thinking which tense to use.
> • Watch out for the personal *a*. It is needed a few times in this translation.

I have known my best friend since I was four years old. I used to admire Mateo because he was loyal and honest. However four months ago I saw Mateo with my girlfriend in a bar. It has been difficult, but last week I met a pretty girl …

> Think about your word order here.

Combining tenses Using more than three tenses together

» Higher p. 169

G
H Even more impressive than using the three past tenses together in your work is being able to add the present and the future tense!

- Use the **present tense** to say what <u>usually</u> happens, what things <u>are</u> like and what is happening <u>now</u> (see pp. 36–49).

- Use the **preterite** to say what someone <u>did</u> (see pp. 50–55).

- Use the **imperfect tense** to say what someone <u>used to do</u>, or for describing things in the past (see pp. 56–57).

- Use the **perfect tense** to say what someone <u>has done</u> (see pp. 70–71).

- Use the **future tense** to say what <u>will</u> happen (see pp. 62–63).

Remember that there are other ways to express future meaning: the near future tense, *esperar* + infinitive, *querer* + infinitive.

Look carefully at the verb endings to help you work out the tense as well as time phrases to give you further clues.

For a reminder of how to form these tenses, look back at the pages mentioned above or refer to the verb tables on pp. 124–128.

H 1   Write which tense matches the descriptions and time phrases.

1   *–aba* and *–ía* endings; *antes …, en el pasado …* ....

2   *haber* + past participle; *durante su vida …* ....

3   no accents except for *vosotros* (you plural); *ahora …* ....

4   infinitive + endings; *mañana …, a partir de ahora …* ....

5   accents except for *nosotros* (we) and irregulars; *ayer …* ....

⭐ Think about the context of the sentence and time phrases for clues.

H 2   Complete this passage with the correct words from the box.

Antes	una vida menos sana.	mucho estrés
y por eso	cigarrillos. Sin embargo	de
fumar y ahora	en forma. El mes pasado	a
correr y este verano	en un triatlón. Espero	
muchos fondos para una organización de caridad.		

empecé
llevaba
recaudar
fumaba
estoy
tenía
participaré
he dejado

3   Complete these translations by putting the verb in brackets into the correct tense and person.

1   They will live together. .... (vivir) juntos.

2   I used to do boxing. .... (hacer) boxeo.

3   He has scored two goals. .... (marcar) dos goles.

4   She ate too much. .... (comer) demasiado.

5   Every day I walk the dog. Todos los días .... (pasear) al perro.

H 4 Translate these sentences into English.

1 A partir de ahora intentaré dejar de fumar porque quiero estar en forma y fumar daña los pulmones.

> Here you need the gerund ('–ing' form) of the verb.

_____

_____

2 Cuando tenía doce años cedió ante la presión de grupo y empezó a tomar drogas blandas, pero ya no fuma porros.

_____

_____

3 Han viajado a muchos países. Por ejemplo, fueron a la India donde vieron muchos festivales religiosos y les encantó la comida.

_____

_____

_____

H 5 Translate these sentences into Spanish.

1 Now I do more sport because I don't want to put on weight. I have already lost five kilos.

> Think about your word order here.

_____

_____

2 I used to buy twenty cigarettes a day but now I will have more money to go out with my friends.

> Irregular stem in the future tense!

> You need _para_ here.

_____

_____

3 They sold their house in England because they hope to rent an apartment in Valencia. It will be perfect for them!

> Do you need _por_ or _para_ if it is for a person?

_____

_____

H 6 Translate this passage into Spanish.

> Irregular past participle!

I have learned a lot here and I have made many friends but next year I will go to another school. I want to be a musician and therefore I need good facilities. Last week I visited a school in Manchester and I really liked it.

> Think: 'it pleased me'.

> You don't need the indefinite article with jobs.

_____

_____

_____

_____

Verb review

G Verbs are the building blocks of any language. Therefore regularly reviewing your understanding of verbs and reminding yourself of useful tips is essential in order to create work that is both accurate and complex.

Complete these exercises on the most common tenses and reflect upon your understanding.

Which tenses are you confident using? Which tenses do you need to revisit and revise? How are you going to become more confident using them?

1 Complete these verb tables and tip boxes.

Present tense

Regular	hablar (to speak)	comer (to eat)	vivir (to live)
(yo)	habl_____	como	viv_____
(tú)	habl_____	com_____	vives
(él/ella/usted)	habla	com_____	viv_____
(nosotros/nosotras)	habl_____	com_____	vivimos
(vosotros/vosotras)	habláis	com_____	viv_____
(ellos/ellas/ustedes)	habl_____	comen	viv_____
Irregular	**ser** (to be)	**salir** (to go out)	**querer** (to want)
(yo)	soy		quiero
(tú)		sales	
(él/ella/usted)			
(nosotros/nosotras)			queremos
(vosotros/vosotras)	sois		
(ellos/ellas/ustedes)		salen	

⭐ If a verb ends in –*mos* the person of the verb is _____.

Stem-changing verb!

⭐ Stem-changing verbs don't change their spelling in the _____ and _____ persons of the verb.

⭐ *salir* is irregular in the *yo* (I) form as it ends in -*go*, just like *poner*, _____ and _____.

Preterite

Regular	viajar (to travel)	beber (to drink)	decidir (to decide)
(yo)	viaj_____	bebí	decid_____
(tú)	viajaste	beb_____	decidiste
(él/ella/usted)	viaj_____	bebió	decid_____
(nosotros/nosotras)	viajamos	beb_____	decidimos
(vosotros/vosotras)	viaj_____	bebisteis	decid_____
(ellos/ellas/ustedes)	viajaron	beb_____	decidieron
Irregular	**ir** (to go)	**tener** (to have)	**hacer** (to do/make)
(yo)	fui		hice
(tú)		tuviste	
(él/ella/usted)			
(nosotros/nosotras)			hicimos
(vosotros/vosotras)	fuisteis		
(ellos/ellas/ustedes)		tuvieron	

⭐ Regular –*er* and _____ verbs have the same endings in the preterite.

⭐ In the preterite, the verbs *ir* and _____ are formed in exactly the same way.

⭐ Irregular verbs in the preterite have no _____.

¡Viva! GCSE Spanish © Pearson Education Limited 2017

H 2 **Complete these explanations of tenses and the tip boxes.**

The future tense

To form the future tense ('will do' something), add the following endings to the _____ of the verb:

–é, _____, _____, **–emos, –éis,** _____.

Some verbs are irregular in the future tense and don't use the infinitive. They have an irregular stem:

hacer – **har**   tener – **tendr**   poder – _____

decir – _____   salir – _____   venir – _____

⭐ The endings are the same for –ar, _____ and _____ verbs.

⭐ All endings in the future tense have an accent apart from _____.

The conditional

To form the conditional ('would do' something), add the following endings to the _____ of the verb:

–ía, _____, _____, **–íamos, –íais,** _____.

The conditional has the same irregular verbs as the _____ tense.

⭐ In the conditional, the endings are the same for _____, –er and _____ verbs.

3 **It's inTENSE! Read the following passage and highlight the verbs in different colours according to your own key of tenses.**

The imperfect tense endings are –aba (–ar verbs) and –ía (–er and –ir verbs), but watch out for irregulars. See pp. 56–57.

El año pasado fui a España con mi amigo. Viajamos en avión porque es rápido y bastante barato. Llegamos a las tres de la mañana y cogimos un taxi del aeropuerto al hotel. El hotel estaba en el centro de Madrid y era un poco ruidoso. Tenía un bar y un restaurante pero no tenía piscina. El año que viene voy a ir a México porque me fascina la cultura y me gusta hablar en español. Mi amigo no puede hablar el idioma, sin embargo dice que va a aprenderlo porque le gustaría volver al país con su novia este verano. Su novia y él estudiarían juntos y yo les ayudaría también. Si vuelve a España, irá a la costa y se quedará en un hotel en la costa porque prefiere tomar el sol y nadar mientras que yo prefiero hacer alpinismo en las montañas.

☐ present
☐ preterite
☐ imperfect
☐ near future
☐ future
☐ conditional

⭐ _____ phrases can give you a clue as to the tense of a verb.

The near future tense uses *ir* (in the present tense) + *a* + infinitive. See pp. 60–61.

4 **Reflect upon your progress and understanding of the different tenses and respond to these questions.**

1 Which tense do you feel most confident using? _____

2 Which tense do you feel least confident using? _____

3 How are you going to improve your understanding and become more confident using that tense?

_____

_____

Here are some useful strategies to help you translate from Spanish into English. As you are doing the translations on the following pages, refer back to these strategies to help you.

Reading for gist

When you are faced with a passage or sentence to translate from Spanish into English, it is really important to read through each sentence in order to establish a general meaning, even if you know that there are some words you don't recognise or cannot immediately translate.

Word order

Remember that word order can be different in Spanish and English.

- If there is an adjective in a sentence, for example, you will need to remember that most adjectives, including all colours, come <u>after</u> the word they describe in Spanish. So, if you had to translate *Llevamos una* **chaqueta negra**, you would write 'We wear a <u>black jacket</u>', not 'a jacket black'.

- Be careful to remember subject pronouns when translating into English. Often you don't need to use them in Spanish because the verb form (usually the ending) makes it clear who is being referred to. So, if you had to translate **Van** *a los Estados Unidos de vacaciones*, you would write '<u>They go</u> to the United States on holiday', because *van* is the third person plural form of the present tense of *ir*.

- Watch out if there are object pronouns in the sentence that you are translating. These normally come <u>in front of</u> the verb in Spanish.

  Nuestros profesores **nos** *ponen muchos deberes.*   Our teachers give **us** a lot of homework.
  (literally 'Our teachers <u>to us</u> give a lot of homework.')

Object pronouns can also be added to the end of infinitives in Spanish.

  *Mi hermano va a dar***me** *un regalo.*   My brother is going to give **me** a present.

Watch out as you might not immediately recognise the infinitive *dar* with the object pronoun placed at the end – you may think that *darme* means something different! Be especially careful of *la*, *los* and *las* meaning 'her/to her' or 'them/to them' as they will come before the verb and must not be confused with the Spanish words for 'the' (*el/la/los/las*).

  Pablo **la** *quiere.*   Pablo loves **her**. | Don't be tempted to translate *la* as 'the' here. |

Using familiar language, context and common sense

- Try to use familiar language, context and common sense to decode the meaning of words you don't know. In the following sentence, identify the words you <u>definitely</u> know:

  Uso Spotify para descargar música de mis cantantes preferidos.

You probably recognise *Uso Spotify* (I use Spotify), *música* (music) and *mis cantantes preferidos* (my favourite singers). You might also know *descargar*, but if you don't, use the vocabulary you do know to make an informed guess. So far you have 'I use Spotify … music of my favourite singers.' Ask yourself: what makes sense in the context of the rest of the text? Given that there are just two words in Spanish, the English translation will probably only be one or two words, so you wouldn't guess something long like 'to search and find' and it can't be something which you already know the Spanish for, such as 'for listening to'. You might guess the correct answer – 'to download'.

Look at this sentence:

  Pablo **está listo** *para salir.* | Be careful: *ser listo* means 'to be clever' and *estar listo* means 'to be ready'. |

It is really important to read the whole sentence or text in your head before you try to translate, so that you have an idea of the general meaning. This will help you to establish the context. You might know that *listo* has two meanings in Spanish, 'clever' and 'ready', but in this context common sense tells you that only one would work.

Now look at this sentence:

  Fumar cigarrillos es muy malo para la salud.

You should be able to guess *cigarrillos* means 'cigarettes' and you've understood the meaning of *malo* ('bad'). So *fumar* and *para la salud* may be words that you don't know but from your general knowledge and common sense you might work out that they mean 'smoking' and 'for your health'.

Using cognates and near cognates

- Look for <u>cognates</u> (words which are the same in both languages, e.g. 'animal', 'perfume', 'hotel') or <u>near cognates</u> (words which are very similar in both languages, e.g. *biología* (biology), *comenzar* (to commence), *difícil* (difficult)) as you can easily work out the meaning of these words in English, even if you might not have known the word if you had been asked to translate it from English into Spanish.
- You can sometimes work out the meaning of a word which is a near cognate and then adapt it to get a better translation.

    Tengo miedo de las serpientes.

    'Serpents' is also an English word, but a more natural translation here would be 'I am afraid of snakes'.

False friends

- Watch out for '<u>false friends</u>': Spanish words which look similar to English, but actually have totally different meanings. Look at these sentences:

    *Mi hermana es muy **sensible**.*   *No me gustaría ser **bombero**.*   *Manú trabaja en una **librería**.*

    If you think about cognates or near cognates, you might have tried the following translations:

    My sister is very **sensible**.   I wouldn't like to be a **bomber**. Manú works in a **library**.

    All three would be wrong! The correct translations are:

    My sister is very **sensitive**.   I wouldn't like to be a **fireman**. Manú works in a **bookshop**.

Grammar

- Use **tense indicators** and your <u>grammatical knowledge</u> to help you translate into the correct tense:

Present: ***Normalmente* <u>vamos</u>** a Grecia en verano.   **Normally** <u>we go</u> to Greece in summer.
Past: ***Ayer* <u>compré</u>** un nuevo móvil.   **Yesterday** <u>I bought</u> a new mobile phone.
Future: ***El año que viene*, mi hermana <u>irá</u>** a Italia.   **Next year** my sister <u>will go</u> to Italy.

- Remember that you can translate some tenses in more than one way. Try out the various versions and see which sounds better in the context:

Present: ***Lleva*** un jersey verde. ➔ He wears a green jumper <u>or</u> He is wearing a green jumper.
Imperfect: ***Estudiaba*** dibujo.   ➔ I studied art <u>or</u> I was studying art <u>or</u> I used to study art.

Translation skills

- Don't always try to translate word for word. This can cause real problems, as you won't always find that one word in Spanish means one word in English.

    Suelo hacer de canguro los viernes.   I usually babysit on Fridays.

    Suelo ➔ I usually   *hacer de canguro* ➔ babysit   *los viernes* ➔ on Fridays

- Sometimes you might have to <u>paraphrase</u> (find a phrase that has the same meaning, but uses different words) to complete a translation that sounds natural in English.

    Nos hace falta papel higiénico en el baño.

    Here, a great translation in English would be 'We need some toilet paper in the bathroom'. A word for word translation would sound very strange in English: 'For us it is missing toilet paper in the bathroom.'

- Don't be afraid to use <u>different words</u> or a <u>different number of words</u> to get a good translation, but don't stray too far from the meaning or make random guesses.

    It is, however, important <u>to account</u> for every word in a translation, even if some words don't need translating or if you need to add words for the sentence to make sense.

    Look at this example:

    *Jugaba **al** baloncesto los fines de semanas.*   He used to play basketball **at** the weekend.

- Make sure that you read your translation to yourself (out loud if you can) to check that it makes sense and sounds natural. For example, you could translate *Odio también llevar uniforme* as 'I also hate wearing uniform' or 'I hate wearing uniform too', but not as 'I hate also wearing uniform', as this sounds clumsy in English. Play around with the word order until your English translation sounds natural.

1a Read this text about the pop group Kiko and Shara.

> This word in Spanish needs multiple words in English.

Kiko y Shara son un dúo musical y son hermanos. Nacieron en Cádiz, en el sur de España. Kiko es muy guapo y es más alto que su hermana. Lleva barba. Shara tiene el pelo más largo que su hermano y es muy simpática y optimista.

> You will need to remember how to translate comparatives with this phrase.

> *Llevar* normally translates as 'to wear', but here you will need to choose a word that works with 'beard'.

b Translate the following words into English.

1 nacieron ....
2 sur ....
3 guapo ....
4 barba ....
5 pelo ....
6 simpática ....

c Now translate the whole text into English.

> 💡 Remember that near cognates can help you translate words. For example, *optimista* means 'optimistic' in English.

....
....
....
....

2a Read this text about Manú and social networks.

Mis amigos y yo usamos Instagram para compartir fotos porque es muy fácil de usar. Uso Spotify porque es la mejor aplicación para descargar la música que me gusta. A mi madre le encanta usar Skype. Ayer habló con su padre, que vive en Estados Unidos.

b Someone has translated the passage but has made mistakes. Correct the errors.

My friends and I use Instagram to ~~download~~ .... photos because it is ~~free~~ ....
to use. I use Spotify because it is ~~a good~~ .... app to ~~share~~ .... music that
I like. My mother ~~likes~~ .... using Skype. Yesterday she talked to her ~~parents~~ ....
who lives in the ~~United Kingdom~~ ....

3 Translate these passages into English.

1 Tengo muchos pasatiempos porque soy muy deportista. Hago footing todos los días. La semana pasada hice equitación con mi mejor amigo. El jueves que viene, voy a jugar al baloncesto con mi equipo y ¡vamos a ganar!

....
....
....

2 Suelo escuchar la música de Adele o Rhianna. Me ayuda a relajarme. Pienso que Rhianna es más guapa que Adele. Esta semana, he comprado el nuevo álbum de Rhianna. ¡Es genial! Tiene una voz preciosa.

....
....

H 4a Read this text about the festival El Correfoc.

> El Correfoc se celebra en otoño en Cataluña. Muchas personas se disfrazan de demonios y desfilan por las calles corriendo, bailando y saltando entre fuegos artificiales. Algunas personas, sobre todo los padres, se han quejado de esta tradición porque dicen que es muy peligrosa. Las autoridades deberían hacer más para proteger a sus hijos, pero tienen cada vez menos dinero para la seguridad.

Check the tense of each verb by looking carefully at the ending.

b Now complete this translation of the text by filling in the gaps.

Correfoc is **1** _____ in **2** _____ in Catalonia. Many people **3** _____
as devils and **4** _____ the streets **5** _____, dancing and **6** _____
between the **7** _____. Some people, **8** _____ parents, **9** _____
about this tradition because **10** _____ is **11** _____. The authorities
12 _____ more to **13** _____, but they have **14** _____ money
for security.

H 5 Translate these passages into English.

Read your translation back to make sure that it is logical and makes sense. Don't forget to check your grammar, spellings and punctuation in English, too!

1 Ricky Martin es un buen modelo a seguir ya que lucha contra la pobreza y por los derechos de los homosexuales. Además, ha hablado abiertamente de su sexualidad, inspirando a muchos jóvenes. Ha hecho mucho para combatir la injusticia y quiere que el matrimonio gay sea legal en su propio país.

_____

_____

_____

2 La paella es el plato más conocido de España, pero si preguntaras a muchos españoles no sabrían su origen. La paella fue inventada hace mucho tiempo por la gente que vivía en el campo y sigue siendo popular en los hogares españoles. Además, podemos comerla en todos los sitios turísticos de España.

_____

_____

_____

3 Mi amiga Lucía fue de compras, ya que sus padres le regalaron mil euros para su cumpleaños. A Lucía le encanta estar a la moda, y por eso se compró un anillo que era muy caro. Lucía había gastado un montón de dinero cuando salió de la joyería. Me dijo que cuando tenga dieciocho años pedirá más dinero.

_____

_____

_____

1 Read this passage about Argentinian holidays and complete the partial translation below.

> En Argentina vamos de vacaciones de verano en diciembre y enero.
> A mis amigos y yo nos gusta hacer deportes acuáticos. Suelo ir a la
> playa con mi hermana y nadamos en el mar. ¡Qué divertido!

Remember to look closely at which tense is used at the start to ensure that you put the translation in the correct tense.

Think carefully when translating *gustar* – look at the pronoun before it so that you know who the subject of the verb is.

In Argentina _we go_ on our _summer_ holiday in December and January. My friends and I _like_ to do _water sports_ . I _usually go_ to _the beach_ with my sister and _we swim_ in the sea. What _fun_! 8/8

Remember that in Spanish you need to look at the end of the verb to decide which person and tense is being used.

2 Read this text about Pablo's holiday. Complete the translation by matching up the sentence halves.

> El año pasado fui a Bilbao con mis padres. Visitamos a unos amigos que viven allí. Alquilamos un piso en el
> centro de la ciudad. Es más barato que quedarse en un hotel. Lo pasé fenomenal.

1 We rented
2 Last year I went to Bilbao
3 We visited
4 I had
5 It's cheaper than

a some friends who live there.
b a flat in the centre of town.
c staying in a hotel.
d with my parents.
e a fantastic time.

3 Translate these passages into English.

1 Vivo en un pueblo industrial en el sur de Perú. Hay mucho tráfico y pocos espacios verdes. Siempre está
sucio, pero lo bueno es que mis amigos viven aquí. Me gustaría vivir en el campo en el futuro.

I live in an industrial town in the south of Perú. There's a lot of traffic and little green space. It also is always dirty, but the good thing is that my friends live here. I would like to live in the countryside in the future. 10/12

2 Valencia es una ciudad que está situada al lado del mar. Hay muchas actividades para los turistas y a los
visitantes les gusta probar platos típicos españoles. Siempre hace más calor en verano que en invierno.

Valencia is a city that's situated by the sea. There are many activities for tourists and for visitors they like tasting eating typical Spanish dishes ~~Spanish dishes~~. It's always hotter in summer than in winter. 11/12

H 4 **Read this text about the Spanish festival of *La Tomatina*. A student used an online translator to translate it. Can you correct the errors?**

> Creo que es muy importante conocer otras culturas cuando se va de vacaciones. El año pasado asistí a una fiesta que se llama La Tomatina donde había una gran batalla de tomates. Solo llevábamos pantalones cortos o trajes de baño. Tiramos un montón de tomates en una hora. Desafortunadamente, había muchos chubascos y no se despejó hasta la noche.

> Remember to leave the names of festivals or Spanish cities in the original Spanish. They almost never change – *Sevilla*, which changes to 'Seville', is the exception!

I think it's very important to ~~meet~~ 1 _get to know_ other cultures when going on ~~vacation~~ 2 _holiday_ Last year I attended a festival called *La Tomatina* where there was a ~~grand~~ 3 _big_ tomato battle. We only ~~wear~~ 4 _wore_ shorts or bathing suits. We ~~throw~~ 5 _threw_ a lot of tomatoes in an hour. Unfortunately, there were a lot of showers and ~~took~~ 6 _it didn't clear up_ until the evening.

S: 5/6

Beware of online translating tools. Always use an online dictionary or app to check meaning.

H 5 **Translate these passages into English.**

1 Si te gusta la vida tranquila y las vistas preciosas, Formentera es el lugar ideal para vivir. Solo se puede llegar a la isla en barco desde Ibiza. Esta inaccesibilidad la convierte en un lugar para escapar del estrés. No hay hora punta en la isla porque casi todos los vehículos están prohibidos.

If you like the tranquil lifestyle and beautiful views, Formentera is the ideal place to live. You can only go on an island, on a boat from Ibiza. This inaccessibility makes it a place to escape stress. There is no rush hour on the island because almost all vehicles are prohibited.

12/12

2 La mejor manera de conocer Madrid es explorar en Segway. Visité la ciudad hace dos años y exploré la historia, los edificios y los monumentos madrileños. Había recorridos de dos o cuatro horas con guías expertos que hablaban al menos dos idiomas. Es importante que traigas tu cámara para sacar fotos. El viaje fue inolvidable gracias a estas experiencias.

The best way to explore Madrid is by Segway. I visited the city two years ago and explored the history, buildings and monuments of Madrid. There were tours of two to four hours with guides experts who speak at least 2 languages. It's important to bring your camera to take photos. The trip was unforgettable thanks to these experiences.

9/12

3 Si tengo la oportunidad en el futuro, iré a la isla más grande del Caribe, Cuba. Por la mañana, escucharía a los músicos que tocan salsa en las plazas o las calles estrechas, o conduciría los coches estadounidenses de los años cincuenta. Por la tarde, tomaría el sol en las playas blancas de Varadero.

If I have the opportunity in the future, I will go to the biggest island in the caribbean, cuba. In the morning, I would listen to the musicians who play salsa in the squares or narrow streets, or I would drive American cars that they drove in the 80's. In the afternoon I would sunbathe on the white beaches of Varadero.

10/12

1 Read this passage from a magazine and complete the partial translation below.

Ir al colegio en Chile

Daniela, 16 años, nos cuenta…

"Estudio en un instituto en Santiago, la capital de Chile. Las clases empiezan a las ocho y acaban a las tres. Mi asignatura preferida es la educación física, pero lo que menos me gustan son las matemáticas. Lo mejor es que las vacaciones de verano duran tres meses, ¡de diciembre a marzo!"

> When translating the definite article *las* you can often miss it out in English so *Las clases* translates as 'Classes'.

> If you are unsure of a translation, look at the other words around it to help you work out its meaning.

> Think about the superlative here.

1 .... at a school in Santiago, the capital of Chile. 2 .... start at eight and 3 .... at three. My favourite 4 .... is PE, but what I like 5 .... is maths. The best thing is that 6 .... last for three months, from December to March!

2 Read this passage and choose which is the correct translation.

Mi nuevo profe de dibujo es mucho más simpático que nuestro profe del año pasado, el señor López. El señor López nos ponía muchos deberes y siempre era demasiado estricto. Nunca aprendí nada y saqué malas notas.

> Always pay attention to negative phrases as they will change the meaning completely if not translated accurately.

a	My new teacher of drawing is nicer than our teacher last year, Mr. Lopez. Mr. Lopez put us many duties and was always too strict. I never learned nothing and got bad grades.
b	My new art teacher is less nice than our teacher from last year, Mr Lopez. Mr Lopez gave us too much homework and was too strict. I never learnt anything and I got rubbish grades.
c	My new art teacher is much nicer than our teacher from last year, Mr Lopez. Mr Lopez gave us a lot of homework and was always too strict. I never learnt anything and I got bad grades.

3 Translate these passages into English.

1 Mi asignatura preferida son las matemáticas porque me encanta resolver problemas. Soy la mejor de la clase y siempre saco buenas notas en las pruebas. Voy a participar en un concurso de matemáticas y espero ganar.

....

....

....

....

> When you have finished the translation, read it aloud to make sure that it sounds natural. If it doesn't, try playing with the word order.

2 Odio mi uniforme. Tengo que llevar unos pantalones grises y una chaqueta del mismo color. Pienso que es feo y demasiado formal, pero mis padres dicen que el uniforme mejora la disciplina y da una imagen positiva de nuestro instituto.

....

....

....

....

H 4 Read this passage and then number the phrases below from 1-8 to put the translation in the correct order. Beware! There are sentences which are incorrect translations.

> Remember to pay close attention to numbers and, in particular to 2 and 12, 3 and 13, and 60 and 70 which can be easily confused.

> La telesecundaria es un modelo de educación en México que empezó en mil novecientos sesenta y ocho. Tiene el objetivo de dar clases a los estudiantes de los pueblos rurales mexicanos a través de programas de televisión. El gobierno quiere mejorar la enseñanza de los niños pobres que no saben ni leer ni escribir.

that started in 1968.		to give classes to students in rural Mexican cities	
through TV programmes.		*Telesecundaria* is an education model in Mexico	
It's objective is		that started in 1978.	
by appearing in TV shows.		improve the education of poor children	
who don't know how to read or write.		It has the object of	
who want to learn to read and write.		make bigger the education of poor children	
The government wants to		to teach students in rural Mexican villages	

> 💡 Avoid translating word for word. Read the whole passage through to get a sense of the overall meaning and make your translation read as though it had originally been written in English.

H 5 Translate these passages into English.

1 Toco la batería desde hace trece años. Me chifla la música rock porque te enseña a improvisar y es súper divertido. El julio pasado dimos un concierto para nuestros compañeros de clase y yo toqué un solo de batería. ¡Fue un éxito! El próximo trimestre, aprenderé a tocar el piano también.

2 En mi escuela primaria no había ni pizarras interactivas ni aulas de informática. La verdad es que el edificio no era adecuado. Ahora estoy más contento en mi nuevo instituto, que tiene mejores instalaciones, porque sé que tendré más oportunidades en el futuro para ir a la universidad y encontrar un buen empleo.

3 Mi instituto tiene demasiadas reglas y no estoy de acuerdo con ellas. Ayer comí chicle en clase y el profesor me castigó. El director no me permitirá ir al parque temático con mi clase al final del año. No creo que sea justo y tengo muchas ganas de salir de este instituto. ¡Lo odio!

1a Read this passage about María's mother and translate the Spanish words below into English.

> Mi madre era azafata y le gustaba su trabajo. Lo bueno era que visitaba muchos países en el extranjero. Visitó los Estados Unidos y Nueva Zelanda diez veces. Lo malo fue que los clientes eran antipáticos.

1 azafata ....

2 visitaba ....

3 muchos países ....

4 visitó ....

5 antipáticos ....

> Read aloud what you have written. If it doesn't sound right to you, it probably isn't.

b Now translate the whole passage into English.

....

....

....

....

2 Read this passage about Sonia and correct the translation below. The mistakes have been crossed out.

> Sometimes words can have two meanings: *trabajo* can mean both 'job' and 'I work'. Look carefully at the context to work out the meaning.

> Be careful here as possession is expressed differently in Spanish and English.

> Trabajo en el restaurante griego de mi tío. Lo odio porque suelo estar en la cocina lavando los platos. Mi tío siempre me da las peores tareas. No voy a trabajar allí en el futuro porque me gustaría ser diseñador.

I work in my **1** ~~aunt's Italian café~~ .... I hate **2** ~~them~~ .... because I **3** ~~stay~~ .... in the kitchen **4** ~~cooking~~ .... My uncle **5** ~~never~~ .... gives me the **6** ~~best~~ .... jobs. I am not going to **7** ~~job~~ .... there in the future because I **8** ~~wanted~~ .... to be a **9** ~~drawing~~ ....

3 Translate these passages into English.

1 Ayudo a mis padres en casa porque ellos siempre están ocupados. Hago de canguro de mi hermana cuando quieren salir. Me dan trece euros cada vez que lo hago. También paseo al perro los fines de semana.

> Take care with little words like *me* and *lo* which can have several meanings.

....

....

....

....

2 Para mis prácticas laborales pasé dos semanas en un banco. La gente del banco era muy simpática, pero trabajaba muchas horas. No voy a volver a trabajar allí en el futuro, y por eso fue una experiencia inútil.

....

....

....

....

H 4 **Read this passage and complete the partial translation below.**

> Trabajar en la moda siempre ha sido mi sueño. Por eso, pasé tres semanas en una tienda de ropa. Solía ayudar a los clientes y el último día mi jefe organizó una fiesta de despedida para mí. Mis padres quieren que vaya a la universidad, pero sé que me gustaría montar mi propio negocio de moda.

> Make sure you are familiar with the present subjunctive when translating this phrase.

Working in **1** _____ has always **2** _____ my dream. Therefore, **3** _____ three weeks in a clothes shop. **4** _____ help customers and on the last day **5** _____ organised a **6** _____ party for me. My parents **7** _____ to go to university, but I know that I would like to **8** _____ my own **9** _____.

> Look at the words surrounding unfamiliar words. They might help you to make a logical guess about which English word would fit in that sentence.

H 5 **Translate these passages into English.**

1 Hice mis prácticas laborales en un zoo. Pasé quince días muy felices allí y tuve mucha suerte porque en el futuro me encantaría trabajar con los animales. Mis compañeros eran agradables y me dieron mucho apoyo. Aprendí a trabajar en equipo y los animales me hacían reír cada día con su comportamiento.

_____

_____

_____

_____

2 En el pasado, muchas chicas iban a España para trabajar de au pair. Vivían con familias españolas y cuidaban a sus hijos. Sin embargo, lo sorprendente es que haya cada vez más chicos que quieren seguir el ejemplo de las chicas para mejorar su conocimiento de la lengua española y ganar dinero.

_____

_____

_____

_____

3 Es importante que aprendamos idiomas. Las lenguas te abren la mente, aumentan tu confianza y mejoran tus perspectivas laborales. Algunas personas dicen que todo el mundo habla inglés y por eso no merece la pena aprender otros idiomas. Posiblemente nunca han ido al extranjero y por eso no saben que las habilidades lingüísticas son muy útiles.

_____

_____

_____

_____

1 Read this passage about protecting the environment and complete the partial translation below.

> El medio ambiente me preocupa mucho y quiero proteger el planeta. Por eso, siempre reciclo el papel y el plástico. En casa, apago las luces cuando salgo de una habitación y siempre me ducho.

Take care when translating reflexive verbs as you don't always translate the reflexive pronoun, e.g. *me acuesto* – I go to bed.

Sometimes you need to translate the infinitive by placing the word 'to' before it.

Make sure you learn linking words like *por eso*, *sin embargo* and *así que*. They are cross-topic words and high frequency.

The environment _____ and I want _____ the planet. _____, I always _____ and plastic. At home, I _____ when I _____ a room and _____ .

2a Read this passage about charity and translate the Spanish words below into English.

> Las fiestas son una excelente idea para recaudar fondos porque es muy divertido estar con tus amigos. Fui a una fiesta para ayudar a la gente de México que sufre a causa de un huracán. Tuve que pagar para entrar.

Remember, in Spanish, unlike English, the word for 'people' takes a singular verb: *la gente es* → people are.

1 recaudar _____   3 divertido _____   5 huracán _____

2 fondos _____   4 ayudar _____   6 tuve que _____

b Now translate the whole passage into English.

_____

_____

_____

3 Translate these passages into English.

1 La sequía es uno de los problemas medioambientales más serios de nuestro mundo. Para informar a la gente, la semana pasada organizamos un festival de música. Muchos músicos y cantantes participaron. Fue genial.

_____

_____

_____

_____

2 En Madrid en verano hace mucho calor y eso afecta a muchas personas. El año pasado, murieron más de cien personas a causa del calor. También, había mucha contaminación por los coches. Va a ser peor en el futuro.

_____

_____

_____

H 4 **Read this passage and then number the phrases below from 1-9 to put the translation in the correct order. Beware! There are sentences which are incorrect translations.**

> Las ventas de pasteles son muy populares para recaudar fondos. Tengo muy buenos recuerdos de las ventas de pasteles cuando estaba en el instituto. Se puede pedir a varias personas que donen distintos productos como pasteles y galletas, para venderlos. Si todo el mundo hiciera algo, no habría tanta pobreza en el mundo.

The passage uses the imperfect tense here.

When making a hypothetical suggestion using 'if' we use the imperfect subjunctive followed by the conditional.

Cake sales are popular for funds.		like cakes and biscuits	
I have very good souvenirs of cake sales		that you can then sell.	
there wouldn't be as much poverty in the world.		when I was at school.	
Cake sales are very popular for fundraising.		If everyone did something,	
I have very good memories of cake sales		to sell them.	
when I am at school		there will be less poverty in the world.	
to donate different products		You can ask several people	

Remember, when translating from Spanish to English you often leave out definite articles.

H 5 **Translate these passages into English.**

1 Hace más de cuarenta años, un pequeño grupo de médicos y periodistas fundó la organización humanitaria 'Médicos sin fronteras'. Ayudan a la gente que es víctima de catástrofes, como inundaciones o terremotos. Ha hecho más de un millón de consultas médicas este año y se estima que habrá más en el futuro.

2 El año pasado hubo una gran inundación en mi pueblo. Una noche, estaba durmiendo, y de repente me desperté porque el agua estaba entrando en mi habitación. Tuve miedo. Para ayudar a las víctimas de este desastre natural, hay que recaudar fondos y se debería solicitar donativos de otros paises.

3 Mi padre decidió comprar contenedores para separar la basura en casa. Siempre hemos querido hacerlo y aprovecharemos la oportunidad para ser una familia ecológica. Sin embargo, el pasado jueves mi padre se enfadó porque mi hermano no se había acordado de utilizar los contenedores. Dijo que estaba demasiado ocupado. En el futuro tendrá que acordarse.

There are some different strategies to consider when you are translating from English into Spanish, partly because you will be able to understand the text you see so you don't need to try to work out any meanings before you start. However, most people would consider that translating into Spanish is more difficult.

When you have a passage or sentence to translate into Spanish, read the whole thing through once. Then work sentence by sentence or phrase by phrase bearing the following strategies in mind.

 Grammar

Verbs

- Think carefully about the verb forms you need. Who is the subject of the verb (who is doing the action)? Is it more than one person? Make sure you know your verb endings.

> When translating verb forms into Spanish you won't normally need to translate the pronouns (I/you/he/she/we/they) as the verb ending will tell the reader who is doing the verb.

We went to Spain.	*Fuimos a España.*
He went to Spain.	*Fue a España.*

Always read the English carefully to make sure you have identified which <u>tense</u> needs to be used in Spanish. Look for clues such as time markers to help you.

Last week, I visited my friend. ➔ <u>preterite tense</u> needed

Next week, she will play tennis. ➔ <u>future tense</u> needed

But remember that to say how long you <u>have been doing/have done</u> something in Spanish, you use *desde hace* + the present tense, when you would use the perfect tense in English. Don't let this catch you out!

We have played tennis for six years.   *Jugamos al tenis desde hace seis años.*

- Take care with <u>reflexive verbs</u> in Spanish as these aren't always obvious from the English. Reflexive verbs are frequent in daily routine translations at GCSE.

I shower every morning.   ***Me** ducho cada mañana.*

- Remember that Spanish uses <u>infinitives</u> when English uses words ending in 'ing'.

> Try to remember which verbs are often followed by an infinitive.

I hate **doing** my homework.   *Odio **hacer** los deberes.*

- You might have to use <u>modal verbs</u>, so look out for 'can', 'must', 'should', 'allowed to' and remember that these verbs are followed by the infinitive in Spanish.

You **should** eat fruit every day.   ***Se debería** comer fruta todos los días.*

Nouns and adjectives

- Gender, articles and adjectival agreement and position are also really important when you are translating nouns into Spanish.

> Remember that the *–o* ending changes to *–a* when the adjective describes a feminine noun and the ending will become *–os* or *–as* when the noun is plural. If the adjective ends in a consonant, it does not change in the feminine singular but you need to add *–es* in the plural.

We have a **small** guinea pig.	*Tenemos una cobaya (pequeña).*
I ate some **delicious** prawns.	*Comí unas gambas (deliciosas).*
She has **brown** eyes.	*Tiene los ojos (marrones).*

Time phrases

- Learn common time and frequency phrases so you always have them ready to use: yesterday (*ayer*), today (*hoy*), tomorrow (*mañana*), every day (*todos los días*), etc.

> Try to remember that *por la mañana* translates as 'in the morning' (and not 'for tomorrow'). You also use *por* with *por la noche* and *por la tarde*.

Useful little words

- Build up your bank of vocabulary with useful little words, which you are likely to need in your translations, for example: <u>intensifiers</u> (quite – *bastante*, very – *muy*), <u>quantifiers</u> (a lot of – *mucho/a/os/as*, a little – *un poco de*), <u>conjunctions</u> (but – *pero*, because – *porque*), <u>prepositions</u> (with – *con*, from – *desde*).

Word order

- You need to think carefully about word order when you are translating into Spanish. Remember the rules for adjectives and object pronouns:

Adjectives

Spain has lots of beautiful beaches.   *España tiene muchas playas **bonitas***.

> Most adjectives, including all colours, come <u>after</u> the noun they describe.

Object pronouns

She has given **us** a present.   ***Nos** ha dado un regalo.*

> The pronoun *nos* comes <u>before</u> the verb.

Remember, when translating verbs such as 'like' and 'love' in English you need to think carefully about how you construct the sentence. For example, 'I like strawberries' would be translated as *Me gustan las fresas*, which literally translates as 'Strawberries are pleasing to me'.

Translation skills

- Be careful with words which we miss out in English but which must be there in Spanish, and vice versa.

I don't like coffee.	*No me gusta **el** café.*
On Sundays he plays football.	*Los domingos juega al fútbol.*
My brother wants to be **a** journalist.	*Mi hermano quiere ser periodista.*

- Avoid translating word for word when you translate into Spanish.
  Be particularly careful with the present continuous in English, which sometimes does not need to be directly translated into Spanish.

I am listening to music.	***Estoy escuchando** música.*
I am studying French at university.	***Estudio** francés en la universidad.*

> Use the present continuous tense for something that you are doing right now.

Similarly, the imperfect tense in Spanish is a single word.

I used to play tennis. / **I was playing** tennis.   ***Jugaba** al tenis.*

The same is true for 'will' in the future tense and 'would' in the conditional. They are not separate words in Spanish.

We will go to Tenerife in winter.   ***Iremos** a Tenerife en invierno.*

She would work in an orphanage.   ***Trabajaría** en un orfanato.*

- We are sometimes a little lazy with our written English, but Spanish does not allow this.

The city I visited…   *La ciudad **que** visité…*

> In English a more correct way to say this would be 'The city that I visited', and *que* is needed here in Spanish.

- When you are asked to translate from English into Spanish, you might need to look carefully at the sentence or part of the sentence which comes <u>before</u> the one you are translating.

Last year we bought a house in Spain. It is too small and very noisy.

El año pasado compramos una casa en España. Es demasiado pequeña y muy ruidosa.

> The noun '*casa*' comes before the adjectives which describe it. Because it is a feminine noun you need to change the endings of the adjectives to agree.

- If you don't know how to say something in Spanish, don't panic! Try to think of a synonym, a similar word, or another way to say it using vocabulary that you <u>do</u> know.

- Check your spelling, accents and grammar!

- If you have time, it is a good idea to try to translate what you have written back into English, to see if it really does match the translation you were asked to do.

⭐ As you are working through the translations on the following pages, try to avoid using translation software, lots of which is available online. Although online dictionaries can be helpful for individual nouns, there is no guarantee that any online translation service can provide you with a correct answer in any context. Don't just accept the first answer you find!

Look at this sentence in English and its Spanish translation. Try to see how the translation was made.

Note that after verbs of liking/loving/hating the second verb must be in the infinitive.

I love playing basketball because it is fun.
Me encanta jugar al baloncesto porque es divertido.

Adjectives must agree with the noun that they describe.

Remember *jugar* is followed by the preposition *a*.

Remember that you don't translate 'it' and 'is' separately. The verb conjugation lets the reader know who is doing the action.

1 Translate these sentences into Spanish. The first four have been partially translated to help you.

1   I like to play chess with my friends.

Me gusta jugar al

2   At weekends, she chats and sends messages on her mobile.

Los fines de semana

3   I often read magazines but I never read poetry.

Leo revistas a menudo, pero

4   He will never share his photos because it is dangerous.

Nunca compartirá sus fotos

5   Last week, I watched a reality show and it was very funny.

6   I get on well with my best friend.

7   Last night he fought with his sister.

8   Yesterday we played volleyball on the beach.

9   She is going to buy a hat for her sister's wedding.

10 Tomorrow, I will use Skype to contact my family in Ireland.

H 2 Read this passage and complete the partial translation below.

> When you translate 'I think' in Spanish you always need the word for 'that' even though in English we can leave it out.

> You will need to think about adjectival agreement to make sure your spellings are accurate.

I think that many footballers are bad role models because they behave badly on the football pitch. They are often rude and selfish. Sometimes they get drunk and fight. I would like to be a footballer when I am older and I will be a good role model because I will help others and I will raise funds for charities.

> You will need to think about the subjunctive here to conjugate the verb correctly.

1 .... muchos futbolistas son malos modelos a seguir porque se comportan mal en el campo de fútbol. A menudo son

2 .... A veces se emborrachan y

3 .... 4 .... ser futbolista cuando

5 .... mayor y seré un buen modelo a seguir porque ayudaré

6 .... y 7 .... para organizaciones de caridad.

H 3 Now translate these two passages into Spanish.

1 When I was ten I used to play handball, but I no longer play it. Now I am a member of a canoeing club and we train every weekend on a lake near my house. In the future I would like to represent my country in the Olympic Games. I will win more gold medals than Usain Bolt!

> Make sure you check the tense in English so that you choose the correct tense in Spanish.

....

....

....

....

....

> Look at the translation strategies on pp. 112–113 to help you.

2 My best friend is called Pablo and we get on very well. We have known each other for twelve years. He supports me and never criticises me. We love travelling and last summer we went to France together. Next winter I am going to go skiing with my parents and he will come with me.

....

....

....

....

¡Viva! GCSE Spanish © Pearson Education Limited 2017

Look at this sentence in English and its Spanish translation. Try to see how the translation was made.

Last summer, I went to Benidorm and it was sunny.
El verano pasado, fui a Benidorm e hizo sol.

Remember that many weather expressions in Spanish are formed using the verb *hacer*. Make sure you look back at irregular tense verb formation on pp. 38 and 52.

Remember that before words beginning with 'i' and 'hi' (when the sound is 'ee') the word for 'and' is *e*.
e.g. *Hablo español e italiano.*
    Padre e hijo.

1 Correct these translations.

1 Next winter, I will go to Sweden but it will be cold!

El pasado invierno, ir a Suecia, pero ¡hacerá frio!

2 Last April, I went to Wales and it was very windy.

El pasado abril, fue a Gales y hacó mucho veinto.

2 Translate these sentences into Spanish.
The first four have been partially translated to help you.

Break each sentence down into small, manageable and logical chunks and think carefully about spellings and accents.

1 I live in Leeds in the north of England.

Vivo en Leeds

2 During her holidays, she likes to swim in the sea.

Durante sus vacaciones,

3 I prefer living in the countryside because it is peaceful.

Prefiero vivir en el campo porque

4 We hate holidays in England because it's always bad weather.

Odiamos las vacaciones en Inglaterra porque

5 Next year we're going to go to the south of France with our grandparents.

6 Every day my friend and I go to the park in our town.

7 I would like to visit Italy because my mother is Italian.

8 You can go shopping in the *Gran Vía* in Madrid.

9 They went to Barcelona and they saw a match at the Camp Nou stadium.

10 When I visited Mallorca I lost my sunglasses on the beach.

H **3** **Read this passage and complete the partial translation below with the correct word or phrase.**

Remember that the word 'many' must agree with the noun it qualifies.

Remember, when translating 'would' you need to use the conditional tense.

Many British tourists go to the south of Spain for its beautiful beaches but the north of Spain has many also. I would like to visit Santander because you can spend lots of time in the open air or sail on the sea. Next year, there will be a flight from Manchester if you want to visit this interesting region.

Muchos turistas británicos **1** .... al sur de España por sus

2 .... playas, pero el norte de España **3** .... también.

4 .... visitar Santander porque se puede pasar **5** ....

tiempo **6** .... o **7** .... en el mar.

El año que viene, **8** .... un vuelo de Mánchester si **9** .... visitar

10 .... interesante región.

⭐ In Spanish, adjectives often follow the noun but sometimes they are placed before the noun.

H **4** **Translate these passages into Spanish.**

1 Last year, I visited Croatia with my school and we had a fantastic time. The people are friendly and there are many activities for young people. My aunt says that it is not a safe country, but I do not believe her. My dream would be to live there.

....

....

....

....

2 Tenerife is one of the most popular Canary Islands. It is close to the African coast and it is always sunny and warm. It takes four hours to reach the island by plane from England. Last year they opened a new water park and my friend Pablo has told me that he wants to go.

....

....

....

....

....

💡 Look at this sentence in English and its Spanish translation. Try to see how the translation was made.

> I wear a grey skirt and a white blouse.
> *Llevo una falda gris y una blusa blanca.*

Adjectives usually come <u>after</u> the noun in Spanish.

The adjective is feminine and singular. It agrees in gender and number with the noun *blusa*.

1 Complete these English sentences and their Spanish translations.

e.g.	I don't like geography because it is boring.	No me gusta la geografía porque es aburrida.
1	On Mondays at 12.15 _____.	_____ tengo inglés.
2	My uniform _____ and comfortable.	_____ es elegante _____ .
3	_____ blue _____ and a _____ shirt.	Llevo pantalones _____ negra.

2 Translate these sentences into Spanish. The first four have been partially translated to help you.

💡 Always check your work to make sure your spellings and verb formations are correct.

1 I go to school by car with my dad.

Voy al instituto

2 Bullying is a problem for my friends at school.

El acoso escolar es un problema

3 My friend Sara sings in the choir when I go to chess club.

_____ cuando yo voy al club de ajedrez.

4 Yesterday, I walked to school with friends but it rained!

_____ con los amigos, ¡pero llovió!

5 Chemistry is more difficult than physics.

⭐ School subjects have articles in Spanish.

6 In my primary school there were fewer students.

7 You are not allowed to use a mobile phone in lessons.

8 We are going to visit a Spanish school next week.

9 If I pass my exams, I will **celebrate** with my parents at home.

You need to say 'celebrate it' in Spanish.

10 My French teacher is the worst in the school.

3 Read this passage and then number the phrases below from 1–9 to put the translation in the correct order. Beware! There are sentences which are incorrect translations.

> Last year we went on an exchange with a school in Zaragoza. We arrived at the airport at three o'clock and all the Spanish families had gone there to meet us. I stayed with Paco and he was very friendly. He didn't speak English so I had to practice my Spanish. I would love to return in the future.

Be careful with object pronouns here.

El año pasado hicimos un intercambio		Me encantaría ir en el futuro.	
Llegué al aeropuerto a las tres		Me encantaría volver en el futuro.	
a buscar nosotros.		a buscarnos.	
Me quedé con Paco y era muy simpático.		No habló inglés	
y todas las familias españolas habían ido allí		con un instituto de Zaragoza.	
No hablaba inglés		así que tuve que practicar mi español.	
Llegamos al aeropuerto a las tres		El año pasadao fuimos en un intercambio	

If you don't know a word in Spanish, try to think of a synonym or similar word. For example, there are two words for 'strict' which could be used in passage 1: *severo* or *estricto*.

4 Translate these passages into Spanish.

1 I hate school because I am very stressed. My teacher is very strict and the worst thing is I have to do a Spanish oral and I am scared. I am worried about my best friend Pablo because bullying is a problem in my school and there are pupils who make fun of him.

2 I hope to pass my exams in the summer because my parents have said they will buy me a new watch if my grades are good. I had a test last week and I thought that I had passed it but I failed! I will talk to my teacher and he will give me strategies to study better.

Look at this sentence in English and its Spanish translation. Try to see how the translation was made.

In order to be a mechanic, I have to do a three-year apprenticeship.

Para ser mecánico, tengo que hacer un aprendizaje de tres años.

When saying what job someone does, you do not use the indefinite article.

Remember that *tener* is an irregular verb and is followed by the infinitive when used with *que*.

1 Unjumble these translations.

1 I'm looking for a job with a good salary.

trabajo/un/sueldo/con/busco/buen/un

2 My brother is a mechanic and repairs cars.

coches/y/es/hermano/mecánico/mi/repara

2 Translate these sentences into Spanish. The first four have been partially translated to help you.

1 My father is a gardener and he has to look after the plants.

Mi padre es jardinero

2 I would like to be a teacher because I love children.

Me gustaría ser profesora

3 She is very ambitious so she wants to be a singer.

Es muy ambiciosa

4 I am going to travel and live abroad in the future.

Voy a viajar

5 My brother went to university in Scotland and studied Modern Languages.

6 Lady Gaga worked as a waitress before being famous.

7 Pablo is going to work as a volunteer in a hospital in South America.

8 It is more interesting working as an actor than being a shop assistant.

9 Sometimes customers are unfriendly and rude in supermarkets.

10 She is going to be an engineer in the future because she loves maths.

H 3 **Read this passage and complete the partial translation below.**

> You will need the preterite here as the time phrase is 'last year'.

> Be careful with accents as they can change the meaning. For example, *trabajo* means 'I work' but *trabajó* means 'he/she worked'.

> Volunteer work increases your self-confidence and allows you to improve your social skills. Last year, my brother worked in an orphanage in Equatorial Guinea. The trip was a success because he could speak a foreign language. Next year, when I am older I will take a gap year in Colombia before going to university.

> Remember *cuando* + a future intention takes the present subjunctive.

> 💡 Use time phrases like 'this weekend', 'last year' or 'next Thursday' to help you decide what tense to use.

El voluntariado aumenta tu **1** _____ y te **2** _____ mejorar

tus habilidades **3** _____ . **4** _____ , mi hermano **5** _____ en un orfanato

en Guinea Ecuatorial. El viaje **6** _____ un éxito porque sabía hablar **7** _____ extranjero.

El próximo año, cuando **8** _____ mayor **9** _____ un año sabático en Colombia **10** _____ ir a

la universidad.

H 4 **Translate these passages into Spanish.**

1 When I am older, I would like to be a hairdresser. I have always wanted to cut hair because I am creative and sociable. My friends think I am crazy because they all want to be famous. My parents want me to go to university, but it costs too much.

_____

_____

_____

_____

_____

2 My sister studied law at the University of Manchester and now she is a lawyer for a company in London. She earns a good salary but she will earn less next year because she is going to have a baby. Her fiancé, Peter, is a businessman; he is loyal and has a good sense of humour.

_____

_____

_____

_____

💡 Look at this sentence in English and its Spanish translation. Try to see how the translation was made.

> I want to protect the planet so I recycle paper and plastic.
>
> *Quiero proteger el planeta, por eso reciclo el papel y el plástico.*

Remember the stem-changing verb *querer*.

Note that in English we miss out the definite article but in Spanish you have to put it in.

Make sure you are familiar with irregular verbs as these are often the most frequently used. Make a poster to put on your bedroom wall to help remember them.

---

1 Translate these sentences into Spanish. The first four have been partially translated to help you.

1 She is environmentally conscious because she separates the rubbish and recycles glass.

   Es ecológica porque

2 We use public transport to reduce pollution in our town.

   para reducir la contaminación en nuestra ciudad.

3 Yesterday I gave ten euros to a campaign to protect the rainforest.

   Ayer di diez euros

4 Our children are going to live in a better world.

   Nuestros hijos

5 My family always buys environmentally friendly products.

6 It is better to walk than to travel by car.

7 The worst problem is the destruction of the environment.

8 We must look after our beautiful planet.

9 You should not waste either water or energy.

10 I watched the World Cup on TV with my best friend Raúl.

H 2 **Read the English passage and correct the Spanish translation below. The mistakes have been crossed out.**

> In many countries you have to pay for a plastic bag in shops. When you go to the till the assistant will ask you if you need one. The campaign to reduce the number of plastic bags was successful in France. I would like to do more to help but I don't know what I should do.

> Think carefully about the form of the verb that follows this 'trigger'.

> Remember that in Spanish the expression 'to be successful' uses the verb *tener* not *ser*.

En muchos países ~~tienen~~ _____ que pagar por una bolsa de plástico en las tiendas. Cuando vayas a la caja, el dependiente te ~~preguntaré~~ _____ si ~~necesitamos~~ _____ una. La campaña para ~~reducer~~ _____ el número de bolsas de plástico ~~era~~ _____ éxito en Francia. Me ~~gusta~~ _____ hacer más para ~~protegir~~ _____, pero no sé lo que ~~deber~~ _____ hacer.

> 💡 Make sure you are familiar with expressions that are formed with the verb 'to be' in English but in Spanish are formed with the verb *tener* ('to have'). e.g. *tener éxito, tener sed/hambre, tener prisa*.

> 💡 Look closely at the English time frames so you choose the correct tense in your Spanish translation.

> Remember, in Spanish there are two verbs, *saber* and *conocer*, for the one English verb 'to know'.

H 3 **Translate these passages into Spanish.**

1 Many Mexican children are dying due to droughts. I had always wanted to help, but I didn't know what I could do. Last week I went to a music festival that was raising funds for children in danger in Mexico. The concert was a success and there will be another next year.

_____

_____

_____

_____

_____

2 Many athletes dream of winning a gold medal at the Olympic Games. When they take place in 2020, Spanish athletes will want to win many medals, especially in gymnastics, sailing and cycling. It is sad that so many competitors take drugs to improve the possibility of winning, but there is pressure to be the best.

_____

_____

_____

_____

_____

Verb tables

Regular verbs

Learn the pattern for –ar, –er and –ir verbs and you can use any regular verbs!

infinitive	pronouns (only include for emphasis)	present	future	conditional	preterite
hablar to speak (regular –ar verb)	yo tú él/ella/usted nosotros/as vosotros/as ellos/ellas/ustedes	hablo hablas habla hablamos habláis hablan	hablaré hablarás hablará hablaremos hablaréis hablarán	hablaría hablarías hablaría hablaríamos hablaríais hablarían	hablé hablaste habló hablamos hablasteis hablaron
comer to eat (regular –er verb)	yo tú él/ella/usted nosotros/as vosotros/as ellos/ellas/ustedes	como comes come comemos coméis comen	comeré comerás comerá comeremos comeréis comerán	comería comerías comería comeríamos comeríais comerían	comí comiste comió comimos comisteis comieron
vivir to live (regular –ir verb)	yo tú él/ella/usted nosotros/as vosotros/as ellos/ellas/ustedes	vivo vives vive vivimos vivís viven	viviré vivirás vivirá viviremos viviréis vivirán	viviría vivirías viviría viviríamos viviríais vivirían	viví viviste vivió vivimos vivisteis vivieron
levantarse to get up (regular reflexive verb)	yo tú él/ella/usted nosotros/as vosotros/as ellos/ellas/ustedes	me levanto te levantas se levanta nos levantamos os levantáis se levantan	me levantaré te levantarás se levantará nos levantaremos os levantaréis se levantarán	me levantaría te levantarías se levantaría nos levantaríamos os levantaríais se levantarían	me levanté te levantaste se levantó nos levantamos os levantasteis se levantaron

Irregular verbs

dar to give	yo tú él/ella/usted nosotros/as vosotros/as ellos/ellas/ustedes	**doy** das da damos **dais** dan	daré darás dará daremos daréis darán	daría darías daría daríamos daríais darían	**di** **diste** **dio** **dimos** **disteis** **dieron**
decir to say	yo tú él/ella/usted nosotros/as vosotros/as ellos/ellas/ustedes	**digo** **dices** **dice** decimos decís **dicen**	**diré** **dirás** **dirá** **diremos** **diréis** **dirán**	**diría** **dirías** **diría** **diríamos** **diríais** **dirían**	**dije** **dijiste** **dijo** **dijimos** **dijisteis** **dijeron**
estar to be	yo tú él/ella/usted nosotros/as vosotros/as ellos/ellas/ustedes	**estoy** **estás** **está** estamos estáis **están**	estaré estarás estará estaremos estaréis estarán	estaría estarías estaría estaríamos estaríais estarían	**estuve** **estuviste** **estuvo** **estuvimos** **estuvisteis** **estuvieron**
hacer to do/make	yo tú él/ella/usted nosotros/as vosotros/as ellos/ellas/ustedes	**hago** haces hace hacemos hacéis hacen	**haré** **harás** **hará** **haremos** **haréis** **harán**	**haría** **harías** **haría** **haríamos** **haríais** **harían**	hice hiciste hizo hicimos hicisteis hicieron
ir to go	yo tú él/ella/usted nosotros/as vosotros/as ellos/ellas/ustedes	**voy** **vas** **va** **vamos** **vais** **van**	iré irás irá iremos iréis irán	iría irías iría iríamos iríais irían	**fui** **fuiste** **fue** **fuimos** **fuisteis** **fueron**

¡Viva! GCSE Spanish © Pearson Education Limited 2017

	imperfect	gerund (for present and imperfect continuous tenses)	past participle	present subjunctive	imperative
hablar (continued)	hablaba hablabas hablaba hablábamos hablabais hablaban	hablando	hablado	hable hables hable hablemos habléis hablen	habla (tú) hablad (vosotros/as)
comer (continued)	comía comías comía comíamos comíais comían	comiendo	comido	coma comas coma comamos comáis coman	come (tú) comed (vosotros/as)
vivir (continued)	vivía vivías vivía vivíamos vivíais vivían	viviendo	vivido	viva vivas viva vivamos viváis vivan	vive (tú) vivid (vosotros/as)
levantarse (continued)	me levantaba te levantabas se levantaba nos levantábamos os levantabais se levantaban	levantando	levantado	me levante te levantes se levante nos levantemos os levantéis se levanten	levántate (tú) levantaos (vosotros/as)

	imperfect	gerund	past participle	present subjunctive	imperative
dar (continued)	daba dabas daba dábamos dabais daban	dando	dado	**dé des dé demos deis den**	da (tú) dad (vosotros/as)
decir (continued)	decía decías decía decíamos decíais decían	**diciendo**	**dicho**	**diga digas diga digamos digáis digan**	**di** (tú) decid (vosotros/as)
estar (continued)	estaba estabas estaba estábamos estabais estaban	estando	estado	**esté estés esté** estemos estéis **estén**	**está** (tú) estad (vosotros/as)
hacer (continued)	hacía hacías hacía hacíamos hacíais hacían	haciendo	**hecho**	**haga hagas haga hagamos hagáis hagan**	**haz** (tú) haced (vosotros/as)
ir (continued)	**iba ibas iba íbamos ibais iban**	**yendo**	**ido**	**vaya vayas vaya vayamos vayáis vayan**	**ve** (tú) id (vosotros/as)

Verb tables

infinitive	pronouns (only include for emphasis)	present	future	conditional	preterite
poder to be able to	yo tú él/ella/usted nosotros/as vosotros/as ellos/ellas/ustedes	**puedo** **puedes** **puede** podemos podéis **pueden**	**podré** **podrás** **podrá** **podremos** **podréis** **podrán**	**podría** **podrías** **podría** **podríamos** **podríais** **podrían**	**pude** **pudiste** **pudo** **pudimos** **pudisteis** **pudieron**
poner to put	yo tú él/ella/usted nosotros/as vosotros/as ellos/ellas/ustedes	**pongo** pones pone ponemos ponéis ponen	**pondré** **pondrás** **pondrá** **pondremos** **pondréis** **pondrán**	**pondría** **pondrías** **pondría** **pondríamos** **pondríais** **pondrían**	**puse** **pusiste** **puso** **pusimos** **pusisteis** **pusieron**
querer to want/wish	yo tú él/ella/usted nosotros/as vosotros/as ellos/ellas/ustedes	**quiero** **quieres** **quiere** queremos queréis **quieren**	**querré** **querrás** **querrá** **querremos** **querréis** **querrán**	**querría** **querrías** **querría** **querríamos** **querríais** **querrían**	**quise** **quisiste** **quiso** **quisimos** **quisisteis** **quisieron**
salir to go out	yo tú él/ella/usted nosotros/as vosotros/as ellos/ellas/ustedes	**salgo** sales sale salimos salís salen	**saldré** **saldrás** **saldrá** **saldremos** **saldréis** **saldrán**	**saldría** **saldrías** **saldría** **saldríamos** **saldríais** **saldrían**	salí saliste salió salimos salisteis salieron
ser to be	yo tú él/ella/usted nosotros/as vosotros/as ellos/ellas/ustedes	**soy** **eres** **es** **somos** **sois** **son**	seré serás será seremos seréis serán	sería serías sería seríamos seríais serían	**fui** **fuiste** **fue** **fuimos** **fuisteis** **fueron**
tener to have	yo tú él/ella/usted nosotros/as vosotros/as ellos/ellas/ustedes	**tengo** **tienes** **tiene** tenemos tenéis **tienen**	**tendré** **tendrás** **tendrá** **tendremos** **tendréis** **tendrán**	**tendría** **tendrías** **tendría** **tendríamos** **tendríais** **tendrían**	**tuve** **tuviste** **tuvo** **tuvimos** **tuvisteis** **tuvieron**
traer to bring	yo tú él/ella/usted nosotros/as vosotros/as ellos/ellas/ustedes	**traigo** traes trae traemos traéis traen	traeré traerás traerá traeremos traeréis traerán	traería traerías traería traeríamos traeríais traerían	**traje** **trajiste** **trajo** **trajimos** **trajisteis** **trajeron**
venir to come	yo tú él/ella/usted nosotros/as vosotros/as ellos/ellas/ustedes	**vengo** **vienes** **viene** venimos venís **vienen**	**vendré** **vendrás** **vendrá** **vendremos** **vendréis** **vendrán**	**vendría** **vendrías** **vendría** **vendríamos** **vendríais** **vendrían**	**vine** **viniste** **vino** **vinimos** **vinisteis** **vinieron**
ver to see	yo tú él/ella/usted nosotros/as vosotros/as ellos/ellas/ustedes	**veo** ves ve vemos **veis** ven	veré verás verá veremos veréis verán	vería verías vería veríamos veríais verían	**vi** viste **vio** vimos visteis vieron

¡Viva! GCSE Spanish © Pearson Education Limited 2017

	imperfect	gerund (for present and imperfect continuous tenses)	past participle	present subjunctive	imperative
poder (continued)	podía podías podía podíamos podíais podían	**pudiendo**	podido	**pueda puedas pueda** podamos podáis **puedan**	**puede** (tú)\n\npoded (vosotros/as)
poner (continued)	ponía ponías ponía poníamos poníais ponían	poniendo	**puesto**	**ponga pongas ponga pongamos pongáis pongan**	**pon** (tú)\n\nponed (vosotros/as)
querer (continued)	quería querías quería queríamos queríais querían	queriendo	querido	**quiera quieras quiera** queramos queráis **quieran**	**quiere** (tú)\n\nquered (vosotros)
salir (continued)	salía salías salía salíamos salíais salían	saliendo	salido	**salga salgas salga salgamos salgáis salgan**	**sal** (tú)\n\nsalid (vosotros/as)
ser (continued)	**era eras era éramos erais eran**	siendo	sido	**sea seas sea seamos seáis sean**	**sé** (tú)\n\nsed (vosotros/as)
tener (continued)	tenía tenías tenía teníamos teníais tenían	teniendo	tenido	**tenga tengas tenga tengamos tengáis tengan**	**ten** (tú)\n\ntened (vosotros/as)
traer (continued)	traía traías traía traíamos traíais traían	**trayendo**	traído	**traiga traigas traiga traigamos traigáis traigan**	**trae** (tú)\n\ntraed (vosotros/as)
venir (continued)	venía venías venía veníamos veníais venían	**viniendo**	venido	**venga vengas venga vengamos vengáis vengan**	**ven** (tú)\n\nvenid (vosotros/as)
ver (continued)	**veía veías veía veíamos veíais veían**	viendo	**visto**	**vea veas vea veamos veáis vean**	ve (tú)\n\nved (vosotros/as)

Verb tables

Here is a list of useful regular –ar, –er and –ir verbs that you can learn:

Regular –ar verbs

aceptar	to accept	enfadarse	to get angry	maquillarse	to put on make up
acompañar	to accompany	enseñar	to teach	mejorar	to improve
aconsejar	to advise	escalar	to climb	nadar	to swim
ahorrar	to save (money)	escuchar	to listen	necesitar	to need
alquilar	to rent/hire	esperar	to hope/wait for	odiar/detestar	to hate
amar	to love	estudiar	to study	olvidar	to forget
arreglar	to tidy	evitar	to avoid	pasar	to spend (time)
ayudar	to help	firmar	to sign	preguntar	to ask
bailar	to dance	fumar	to smoke	presentar	to present
bañarse	to have a bath, to bathe	funcionar	to work (i.e. to function)	prestar	to lend
cambiar	to change			quedarse	to stay/remain
cancelar	to cancel	ganar	to win/earn	quejarse	to complain
cantar	to sing	gastar	to spend (money)	reembolsar	to refund
cenar	to have dinner	gustar (a)/ encantar (a)	to like/to love	rellenar (una ficha)	to fill out (a form)
cepillarse	to brush (teeth, hair)			reparar/arreglar	to repair
charlar	to chat	imaginar(se)	to imagine	repasar	to revise
comprar	to buy	informar	to inform	reservar	to reserve/book
contactar	to contact	intentar	to try	telefonear	to phone
contestar	to answer	interesarse en	to be interested in	terminar(se)	to end
cuidar	to look after	invitar	to invite	tirar (de algo)	to pull (something)
desayunar	to have breakfast	lamentar	to be sorry	tirar	to throw
dibujar	to draw	llamar	to call	trabajar	to work
disfrutar	to enjoy	llamarse	to be called	tratar de	to try to
ducharse	to take a shower	llevarse bien con	to get on well with	usar	to use
durar	to last	mandar	to give orders/to send	visitar	to visit
empujar	to push				

Regular –er verbs

aprender	to learn	esconder	to hide	sorprender	to surprise
beber	to drink	leer	to read	suspender	to fail (an exam)
correr	to run	prometer	to promise	temer	to fear/be afraid
creer	to believe	responder	to answer	vender	to sell
deber	must	romper	to break	ver	to see

Regular –ir verbs

abrir	to open	discutir	to argue	prohibir	to ban, to prohibit
añadir	to add	escribir	to write	recibir	to receive
compartir	to share	existir	to exist	subir	to go up
decidir	to decide	ocurrir	to happen	vivir	to live
describir	to describe	permitir	to allow		

¡Viva! GCSE Spanish © Pearson Education Limited 2017